Words Matter

Words Matter

Embracing the Power of Conversation

Stan H. Wisler

Co-Published with The Association of
School Business Officials

ROWMAN & LITTLEFIELD
Lanham • Boulder • New York • London

Published by Rowman & Littlefield
An imprint of The Rowman & Littlefield Publishing Group, Inc.
4501 Forbes Boulevard, Suite 200, Lanham, Maryland 20706
www.rowman.com

6 Tinworth Street, London SE11 5AL

Copyright © 2019 by Stan H. Wisler

All rights reserved. No part of this book may be reproduced in any form or by any electronic or mechanical means, including information storage and retrieval systems, without written permission from the publisher, except by a reviewer who may quote passages in a review.

British Library Cataloguing in Publication Information Available

Library of Congress Cataloging-in-Publication Data

ISBN: 978-1-4758-4610-2 (cloth)
ISBN: 978-1-4758-4611-9 (pbk.)
ISBN: 978-1-4758-4612-6 (electronic)

Contents

Preface		vii
Acknowledgments		ix
Introduction		xi
1	Words and the Conversation Matter	1
2	Deal with It	13
3	Control Your Emotions	21
4	Create Safe Space	31
5	Speak from the Heart	41
6	Listen for Understanding	49
7	Allow for Differences	57
8	Slow Down	69
9	Reflect	79
10	Create the Win–Win	89
11	Embrace Every Opportunity	99
About the Author		103

Preface

Words have tremendous power. They have the power to build up and create. They also have the power to tear down and destroy. You control which one it will be through the words you use. Words cause an interaction, an interaction creates a conversation, the conversation results in a relationship. Relationships are a key part of our lives.

It is an equation of sorts—the relationship equation. An equation that is applicable to your faith practice, your family relationships, interactions with your friends, and your dealings with work colleagues.

When added together, the components of the equation can result in a positive or negative outcome. It begins with the words. Start with positive, uplifting words and it creates a positive interaction. The positive interaction results in a meaningful conversation, which helps in developing deeper and more satisfying relationships. On the other hand, start with harmful, destructive words and you create a tense interaction, a potentially damaging conversation, and then an awkward, strained relationship. If you start with negative words, each piece of the equation is then directly affected, and the output can be a negative relationship that can negatively affect your life and the life of others.

Careful attention must be given to each step of the cycle. You can't just start with positive words and not pay attention to the interaction or the conversation part of the process and expect the result to be positive. It is similar to a math equation: Start with positive words (+2 points), have a

$$(+/-) \text{ Words} + (+/-) \text{ Interaction} + (+/-) \text{ Conversation} = (+/-) \text{ Relationships}$$

Figure 0.1. The Relationship Equation. *Source*: Illustrated by Austin Wisler

negative interaction (–3 points), and then have a negative conversation (–5 points), and the result is –6 (negative 6) in terms of a relationship [2 + (–3) + (–5) = (–6)].

These concepts apply to electronic communication, that is, texting, e-mailing, and communicating via other types of social media. The interactions and conversations are more one-dimensional. The words become even more crucial since you don't have the benefit of the other aspects of communication, for example, voice inflections, facial expressions, and body language.

Use the principles of conversation outlined in this book to reflect on your own practice, and commit to making improvements where necessary. If you use and consistently practice these guidelines, your interactions and conversations will develop and improve, resulting in deeper and more satisfying relationships.

Acknowledgments

I would like to acknowledge the three most important things in my life: my faith, my family, and my friends. I cherish the relationships that I have benefited greatly from within those three categories.

First and foremost, I am grateful for my faith. My faith has provided an important foundation for my belief system and values. My relationship with a power greater than me has provided order and meaning to my life. It is comforting to know that someone bigger than me has a perfect plan for my life. I had no idea that plan would include writing a book, but I am grateful for the opportunity.

Second, I would like to acknowledge my family. First and foremost, my wife, Donna. She has been an incredible source of support and encouragement throughout our thirty-eight-plus years of marriage. She has been especially patient and understanding during this writing process. I am thankful for the support of my three children, Briana, Eric, and Austin, and their spouses, Jason and Aly. They have been a great source of inspiration. Their belief in me has inspired me to reach higher. I'm also thankful for the great support of my siblings, especially my brother and his wife, Ron and Sharon.

Third, I would like to acknowledge an incredible group of friends and colleagues. I have had many incredible mentors throughout my career from which I have learned a lot. I have enjoyed wonderful relationships with an extraordinary circle of friends who have brought much fun and enjoyment to my life. There are several exceptional friends and colleagues who hold a special place in my heart for the impact they have had on my life and especially this venture. You know who you are. Please accept my sincere thanks.

I would also like to specifically thank Ray Jorgenson, PhD, founder of the Jorgenson Learning Center, who first introduced me to the concepts of the learning conversation. His work is valued and crucial to meaningful and successful leadership. Thank you Ray for the impact you have had on my own leadership.

Introduction

This book is designed to be a resource for individuals who are faced with the task of engaging in crucial conversations. Each chapter describes a specific conversational principle that can be employed to assure a successful result. No two conversations are exactly alike, but these principles are applicable to most, if not all, conversations. The principles are described and supported in each of the chapters.

Although there is no way to guarantee a positive outcome in a challenging conversation, these concepts will provide the tools needed to ensure you have applied maximum effort to the task. Engaging in difficult conversations requires great thought and skill to reach resolution without damaging relationships. These tips will assist you in leading and participating in effective conversations in difficult or stressful conditions, whether in the workplace or in daily life.

Chapter One

Words and the Conversation Matter

> Be mindful when it comes to your words. A string of some that don't mean much to you may stick with someone for a lifetime.
> —Rachael Wolchin

Words are the most common way to communicate a message and express ideas. Although there are other ways of communicating, the use of words is by far the customary method to convey our thoughts, feelings, and intentions. Words are powerful, and their power is used and abused every day. We speak before we think and in an instant create a strained relationship, an uncomfortable situation, and an unrepairable condition. There are key principles that can be employed to guard and protect us from speaking before we think. If you use the conversational principles, you have a greater chance of avoiding uncomfortable, hurtful, and unproductive situations. This book explores those conversational principles.

RELEVANCE AND IMPORTANCE IN TODAY'S COMMUNICATION ENVIRONMENT

The concepts of authentic conversation are relevant in today's environment despite the reliance on other nonverbal forms of communication, for example, e-mailing, texting, and tweeting. In fact, these conversation principles and guidelines are more important than ever as we become more reliant on electronic communication. The lack of exposure to and experience with authentic verbal conversations is increasingly becoming a concern.

Certainly, the concepts and principles of a face-to-face conversation must be modified to fit the technical world of communication, but they are still relevant and important. In the world of texting, e-mailing, and tweeting, the words we use are even more important. In texts, e-mails, and tweets, words are significant and crucial because that is all there is to the message.

The reality of texting and e-mail is that the message is solely reliant on the words that are used. There is no voice tone, body language, facial expressions, or the timing of the delivery to assist in conveying the message. The intended message must be conveyed through one thing—the words. There are emojis that can help, but essentially the words are all you have. You will have to overcompensate with your words. To say that the words matter is truly an understatement.

In the ever-changing world of communication, the face-to-face conversation seems to be missing in the formation, development, and improvement of relationships. Conversations are held through texts and social media channels. Individuals in the same room think nothing of communicating through texts. Difficult and challenging conversations cannot be effectively handled through text or e-mail. Workplace situations cannot be effectively dealt with through text or e-mail. Individuals entering the workforce will need to be aware of and schooled in effective conversational techniques.

NOW MORE IMPORTANT THAN EVER

We are barraged on a daily basis with tweets and other social media posts that contain words that are damaging. Thoughtful and careful consideration should be given to every post. Every post has the potential to reach and impact hundreds, thousands, or even millions of viewers. That incredible impact can be helpful or hurtful.

Even though you may have been very thoughtful and careful with the wording of your post, it may not be received, perceived, or interpreted in the way you intended. Once it is released it is virtually impossible to fully pull it back. Even if you are able to pull it back or edit it, it is likely that many people have already had the chance to see it. The damage may have already been done. In other words, once you hit "share," it is out there for the world to see.

Even in face-to-face conversations, it is impossible to pull back your words. Once it is spoken, the harm may have been done; however, at least in face-to-face conversations, the impact may be limited to one person. There is the possibility and likelihood that that one person will share it with someone. It does, therefore, have the potential to spread but certainly not to the magnitude and extent that a social media post can spread.

WORDS MATTER

Growing up in the 1960s as the fourth of six children, Dan would often hear his parents repeat the phrase "sticks and stones may break your bones, but names will never hurt you." It was their loving attempt to protect him and his siblings from unkind words. Dan never really thought much about the phrase. Dan sort of knew what it meant but did not really think about the message of those words until later on in life.

The phrase "sticks and stones will break my bones but names will never harm me" is an English-language children's rhyme that persuades the child victim of name-calling to ignore the taunt, refrain from physical retaliation, and remain calm. The phrase first appeared in 1862, in the *Christian Recorder*—a publication of the African United Methodist Church. It was presented as an old adage in the form "sticks and stones will break my bones but words will never break me." A majority of the readers of the publication were African American, so it is likely that the phrase was used to give perspective to the name-calling that was prevalent at that time, particularly in the South.

As Dan thought about that phrase, he concluded that the old adage was absolutely untrue and dead wrong. Dan grew up in a very conservative home. His parents were rooted strongly in the traditions of the Church of the Brethren, a conservative Protestant denomination similar to Mennonite. In keeping with the doctrine of the Church of the Brethren, Dan's parents were pacifists. Pacifism is the one practice that sets the Church of the Brethren apart from many other Christian denominations. Pacifism is the promotion of peace. The denomination believes strongly in peaceful resolution in relationships, international conflicts, and treatment of citizens and prisoners.

Most likely the phrase "sticks and stones may break your bones but names will never hurt me" was used by Dan's parents as a way to minimize someone's words or threats to him as a kid and so he did not fight back. As pacifists, Dan and his siblings were taught to "turn the other cheek." It is a noble ideal that is often difficult to enforce and adhere to.

Even though it is all too prevalent today, bullying seemed to be even more prevalent during the mid- to late 1900s. Bullying in schools many times manifested itself in calling other students hurtful and degrading names and words. Hurling insults at fellow classmates was rarely dealt with. The "sticks and stones" phrase was used to send the message that the insults should be discounted and disregarded.

Although there is a greater awareness of bullying in schools today, it is still too prevalent. Many programs have been implemented to eliminate bullying, but it remains a disturbing issue in schools and other places. Social media has not helped, as it is now possible to hurt many more people with one post or text using unkind words. Words are now not just shared between the offender and the offended, they are seen and shared with a much larger audience. The ramifications of those words can have devastating effects. Yes, words can be very hurtful.

As pacifists, the "sticks and stones" phrase may have seemed appropriate to Dan's parents. The idea was that there was no reason to fight back if people called you names or verbally bullied you. The person's words and actions were not causing physical hurt or injury. This is partly wrong. True, the words may not cause a physical injury, but the injuries from words can be much more devastating, damaging, and hurtful than from an actual physical injury. Throughout time, most physical injuries heal. This is not so with injuries created through the words we hear or speak. The damage from words can be irreparable. American author Mary Jessamyn West is quoted as saying, "A broken bone can heal, but the wound a word opens can fester forever."[1]

THE POWER OF WORDS

Think about a time when someone said something to you that had an impact on your life or at least a certain segment of it. You most likely would be able to make two lists of words. One list would be for those words or phrases that individuals have said to you throughout your life that had a positive impact on you. The second list would include words or phrases spoken to you that had a negative impact. It is possible that some of the negative and discouraging words or phrases may have strangely enough had a positive impact on you, but that is certainly the exception and not the rule.

There are cases where negative words have spurred someone on to success. The negative words may have encouraged the individual to prove that the person's words were wrong. There are cases where those negative words were given in the spirit of encouragement and care for the individual; however, there are many situations when those words are given in the spirit of tearing down.

The individual expressing the positive or negative words may have no idea the potential impact they have had or will have. Sometimes the words are received in a way that they were never intended to be. Sometimes the simplest and most common words or statements can have a great impact.

One simple, seemingly silly example of this is something that was casually said to Terry by Carl, who most likely had no idea the impact it would have on Terry. During a time when both Carl and Terry were away from their homes at a professional conference, they were both in the exercise room at the conference resort. Carl was using the weights, and Terry was running on the treadmill. Carl was impressed with Terry's fitness after seeing him run on the treadmill for more than forty-five minutes. As Terry was finishing his run, Carl came over to him and said, "You're a beast." Because of the friendship and relationship they had, Terry knew the context of the comment and knew it was meant as a compliment and an encouragement. For several years after that, when Terry would be training for a race or actually running in a race and struggling a bit, Terry could hear Carl's words in his head—

"You're a beast"—and it would spur him on to keep going. The simplest words matter and have tremendous power.

Words have an impact, sometimes in ways more powerful than ever intended. One powerful word can form or distort someone's view of reality for many years or even a lifetime. There are countless stories of students whose lives have been impacted in a tremendous way through the words of a teacher, principal, or other school employee. The impact of our words is affected by the position we hold as well. If you are in a position of authority, it is likely your words will carry more weight. There are many instances where the words of school guidance counselors have made the difference between a successful college or postsecondary experience and a negative one. In some cases, the student may have decided not to pursue further education because of the words of a parent, teacher, or guidance counselor.

Songs have been written about the impact of words. One that comes to mind is the song "If I Could Turn Back Time," as recorded by Cher. The following are the words of the first part of that song:

> If I could turn back time
> If I could find a way
> I'd take back those words that hurt you
> And you'd stay
> I don't know why I did the things I did
> I don't know why I said the things I said
> Love's like a knife it can cut deep inside
> Words are like weapons, they wound sometimes
> I didn't really mean to hurt you
> I didn't want to see you go

THE PRIMACY EFFECT

Words cannot change reality, but they can change how people perceive reality. In a *Psychology Today* article from the November 2010 publication, the primacy effect is described and demonstrated. The primacy effect is a filter that is created through the words someone uses to describe someone.[2] If a friend introduces you to someone they know and tells you that they are a backstabber and cannot be trusted, you will be on your guard when you talk with this individual. It creates a filter through which you view this person. In the course of the conversation, you will be looking for validation of the characteristic that your friend used to describe this other person.

This effect can be overcome, but it is difficult. You may not even get the chance to overcome the effect. You end up writing off the person before they even have a chance to prove your friend's comment was unjustified.

If a friend introduces you to another person and tells you they are friendly, you will be more likely to cut them a break even if your initial assessment of them is that they did not act very friendly. You may write it off as them having a bad day and give them a second chance. Be aware of the primacy effect as you interact with others.

Remember, words form our perceptions, which shape our beliefs. Our beliefs drive our behavior. Ultimately, this progression from words to perceptions to beliefs to behavior creates the world as we see it.

THE IMPACT OF NEGATIVE AND POSITIVE WORDS

We need to choose and use words carefully and consciously. Despite the fact that all you have to do is look at your own life experiences to validate the differing impacts from positive and negative words, there are individuals who have attempted to prove it scientifically. One such individual was Dr. Masaru Emoto, a Japanese author and entrepreneur, who conducted an experiment to prove the impact of positive words.

He put cooked rice into two different mason jars. He placed them in two different school classrooms and had the students in the one classroom yell "you fool" every time they passed the jar. In the other room, he asked the students to yell "thank you" every time they passed the jar. The jar that contained the rice at which the students yelled "you fool" turned black. The rice in the "thank you" jar stayed white.

This study sounds almost too bizarre to be true, and there are many scientists who refute the studies and question the techniques used. Regardless of its validity, it is intriguing and interesting. There is no question that positive words and thoughts have the potential to constructively alter circumstances and create better conditions than negative words and thoughts. Proof of that premise can be seen through one's own life experiences, as well as through observing the experiences of other people.

TIMING IS IMPORTANT

Using the right words is crucial, but even the right words at the wrong time can be damaging. For example, in the middle of a challenging or difficult situation is not the time to share how the individual could have done something differently.

Many people express uncomfortableness with not knowing what to say at a funeral to an individual who has just experienced loss. We are in fear during those uncomfortable times because we know the potential impact of our words. The uncomfortableness comes from not only not knowing what to say, but also the concern that we may say the wrong thing. For example, the receiving line at the funeral service is not the place to share how you have dealt with heartache from your own personal loss or your suggestions as to how to handle the estate. The conversations may be well meaning, but that is not the right time for them. Carefully consider your words, as well as when might be the right time to share them.

NO WORDS

Words not spoken can be harmful as well. For example, not acknowledging someone's extra efforts can have a negative effect. It can affect an employee's motivation and future performance. Good thoughts do not make a difference until they are verbalized.

Going back to the aforementioned funeral service illustration, not showing up and therefore not offering any words to the grieving party is not the right approach either. If you have experienced the loss of someone close to you or perhaps one or both of your parents, the very fact that someone shows up to the service and/or preservice event is sometimes enough. It means a great deal to know that those who care about you took the time to show up. Their attendance was worth more than any words. Sometimes the less said, the better. A hug or a few words acknowledging their grief may be all that is needed.

FOUNDATIONAL LEADERSHIP BELIEFS

Prior to delving into the details of effective and successful conversations, it may be helpful to share some key leadership concepts. Understanding what is at the core of an effective leadership belief system is important. It will assist you in understanding the basis for the conversational principles and why it is so important to employ the conversational techniques detailed throughout this book.

It is important for you to determine your core belief system. In an attempt to clearly and simply capture your belief system, it is helpful to start by asking why you do what you do and what drives your behavior. A great starting place is to begin by asking, "Why?" Simply put, why do you do what you do? In other words, what makes you tick? Simon Sinek's book *Start with Why* is a great resource to help you with your own "why" statement. The concepts explained in his book are helpful to not only one's professional work life, but also one's personal life. As defined by Sinek, an individual's "why" statement explains the reasons they do what they do. It is the basis for one's actions. Knowing what it is and understanding it is crucial to success.

As an example, my own personal "why" statement, developed after reading Sinek's book, is as follows: "To build relationships and help individuals so that it results in their improved quality of life and success." This "why" statement provides the basis for the strong belief in the power of meaningful conversations. Conversations create and build relationships.

In terms of leadership, the core of effective and truly successful leadership is summed up and described by the concept of servant leadership. As defined by author Robert K. Greenleaf, servant leadership is a philosophy and set of practices that enriches the lives of individuals, builds better organizations, and ultimately creates a more just and caring world. Greenleaf coined the concept of servant leadership in an essay that was first published in 1970. Greenleaf is quoted as saying, "The servant leader is servant first; it begins with the natural feeling that one wants to serve, to serve first."[3]

THE CONVERSATION

Building Relationships

Authentic and meaningful relationships are developed through conversations. Conversation makes the relationship. In the absence of true conversation, a relationship cannot be developed or sustained.

Relationships in life are important to our health and well-being. Life is much more meaningful and fulfilling when it is filled with meaningful and beneficial relationships. Relationships can reduce stress and have been linked to overall improved health.

Harvard University began studying predictors of healthy aging in 1938. Their eighty-plus years of studies span different ages, genders, races, and economic status. The most powerful finding is that individuals who have satisfying relationships are happier, have fewer health problems, and live longer than those who have no or limited relationships. Who among us would not want to enjoy those positive features? So, if relationships are important to the quality of life and conversations make the relationship, then it stands to reason that conversations are important.

An Effective Leadership Skill

To be an effective leader, you need to develop conversational skills. These skills are necessary to build relationships through conversations. The skills related to the art of conversation are needed to effectively deal with challenging, difficult, and uncomfortable situations.

Conversation is an art and not an exact science. There is no one formula for conversational success. Each situation is different. The circumstances and the individuals involved make each occurrence unique, requiring a unique set of skills and approaches. There are some common suggested techniques, but each one must be adjusted and tailored to the situation at hand.

As a leader, you need to be concerned about employee satisfaction. A substantial factor in developing and maintaining satisfied employees is related to the quality of the ongoing conversation. It is good to have satisfied and engaged employees. Satisfied employees assist with accomplishing your organization's goals. Dissatisfied employees can sabotage your goals. Dissatisfied and nonengaged employees can result in lower productivity and higher turnover—all of which is costly to the company. A recent Gallup report states that 63 percent of employees are not engaged in their jobs, while 24 percent are actively disengaged.[4] That means that only 13 percent of employees are engaged in their jobs. These numbers are alarming and should be a wake-up call for employers and leaders to focus on keeping employees engaged, satisfied, and productive.

The key to meeting organizational goals is through the employees. It is important to realize that everyone in an organization has potential. The key is to find the right position and the right place for each person. This is done through conversation. The conversations we have and the words we use have the power to build up employees or bring them down. The goal is to build them up with nurturing words as you help them in their quest to find meaning in their work.

To be an effective leader you need to be able to proactively respond to difficult situations. Responding involves having a conversation. Those conversations have the power to improve or solve the issue. Not having the conversation or having a careless one could make a difficult situation even worse. The ability to have and successfully navigate courageous conversations is a much-needed skill for effective leadership.

Guidelines and Principles for Effective Conversations

The guidelines shared in this book are important components of conversations. The stakes may be serious or low risk, but these concepts should be used in every conversation. Many of these concepts seem to be simple and common sense. Yet, the guidelines outlined and detailed in this book are violated all the time. Make it a point to observe others in conversation, but also look at your own conversational practices. You will see that there is much room for improvement.

It is difficult to adhere to these principles in conversations. Although the concepts seem simple enough, they are difficult to implement, especially on an ongoing and consistent basis. Many are contrary to the way we are naturally wired.

Employing the nine principles described in the following chapters will greatly improve your chances of a positive outcome to any of the difficult situations and confrontations you may be faced with. Perhaps of equal or greater value will be the enrichment of current and future relationships—personal and professional. The nine principles are as follows:

1. Deal with it
2. Control your emotions
3. Create safe space
4. Speak from the heart
5. Listen for understanding
6. Allow for differences
7. Slow down
8. Reflect
9. Create the win–win

If you truly embrace, practice, and use these techniques, the result will be the following:

- Even the most difficult and challenging conversations will be easier and less painful to navigate. There will be a greater chance of a productive, successful outcome to tough situations.
- Authentic and gratifying relationships will be developed and enhanced.
- The techniques will become more natural and require less thought as you continue to practice and use them.

These effective conversational techniques are examined in the chapters of this book.

SUMMARY

The tongue has incredible power. The tongue can be used to bring blessings and an enriched life or curses and demise. Our tongues can be the most difficult part of our body to control, and they often leave us with great regret when we use words to hurt.

The book of Proverbs from the Bible is filled with verses that warn against using our tongues and mouths to speak words that hurt and often cause great turmoil. One such verse is found in Proverbs 15:4 (NIV), where it says, "The soothing tongue is a tree of life, but a perverse tongue crushes the spirit." Another verse, found in Proverbs 21:23 (NIRV), says, "Those who are careful about what they say keep themselves out of trouble."

Never has this subject been more important than now. Reports from media sources inundate us with words that have been spoken, tweeted, e-mailed, posted, or texted that have had far-reaching, unfortunate, and, in some cases, catastrophic implications. We need to be reminded to carefully consider the words we plan to use prior to opening our mouths.

The good news is that we can get better at communicating in a way that builds up others and is positively received. We need to continue to practice and implement thoughtful messaging. And when you fail and your words have been hurtful, you can approach the individual impacted with confidence—knowing that if you employ effective conversational principles, you greatly increase your chances for a positive outcome.

CHAPTER 1 RECAP

- Words are important in all communications—face-to-face conversations, texting, social media posting, and e-mailing.
- It is crucial to choose your words carefully.
- Words have great power—the power to build up or tear down, the power to encourage or discourage, the power to have a long-lasting impact.
- Words said about others can have a big impact—others' interactions can be adversely affected by your comments.
- Choose words that are appropriate for the situation—the right words at the right time.
- Sometimes saying no words may be more appropriate and better than saying a few words.
- The concepts of servant leadership are crucial in effective conversations, interactions, and meaningful relationships.
- Valued relationships are built through effective and authentic conversation.
- Adhering to the principles of good conversation is essential to effective leadership.

NOTES

1. Mary Jessamyn West, quoted in, "Jessamyn West Quotes," AllGreatQuotes, n.d. Accessed July 19, 2019, https://www.allgreatquotes.com/quote-222461/.

2. Jack Schafer, "Words Have Power," *Psychology Today*, November 2, 2010. Accessed June 24, 2019, http://www.psychologytoday.com/us/blog/let-their-words-do-the-talking/201011/words-have-power/.

3. Robert K. Greenleaf, "The Servant as Religious Leader," in *The Power of Servant-Leadership: Essays*, ed. Larry C. Spears (San Francisco, CA: Berret-Koehler Publishers, 1998), 111–68, 123.

4. Steve Crabtree, "Worldwide, 13% of Employees Are Engaged at Work: Low Workplace Engagement Offers Opportunities to Improve Business Outcomes," Gallup, October 8, 2013. Accessed July 18, 2019, https://news.gallup.com/poll/165269/worldwide-employees-engaged-work.aspx.

Chapter Two

Deal with It

Confrontation leads to action. Avoidance leads to inaction.
—Colleen Hoover

One of the first steps to dealing with a difficult situation is to realize you need to deal with it. Perhaps it is the most important and crucial step. Fight the notion that the situation will go away, or that it's really not that bad, or that you do not have the time to deal with it. In other words, the first step is to accept the fact that you need to confront the situation. Realize that you need to deal with it and accept the fact that confronting it really is the best way to handle the situation.

In Stephen M. R. Covey's book *The Speed of Trust*, he demonstrates the value and crucial nature of trust and trusting relationships. Covey outlines and describes thirteen behaviors that increase trust and build trusting relationships. Behavior eight is confronting reality. The concept is similar to the conversation concept "deal with it." Covey says confronting reality is about taking the tough issues head-on. It's about sharing the bad news, as well as the good, naming the "elephant in the room," addressing the "sacred cows," and discussing the "undiscussables."[1]

Most people lean toward conflict avoidance. In general, when people are asked how they deal with conflict, they say that they try to avoid it; however, when those same people are asked whether a strategy of conflict avoidance works, they say it does not work.

There are those who gravitate toward conflict, but if you are one of those people, you are in the minority. There are individuals who thrive on drama, conflict, or difficult situations. In some cases, it may be an example of what could be called the "superhero syndrome." Some people gain self-importance and find their self-worth in the ability to go in and save the day. They exert their power (perceived or real) over the situation and fix it. Just like a "superhero," they fly in and save the day. They may fix the immediate problem and it may give them a sense of power and purpose, but it is not a healthy approach for the organization or the impacted individual(s). Frankly, in many of those situations, they have not actually fixed the problem at all. Yes, the situation has been dealt with and it is crossed off of their to-do list, but it is not really resolved.

If you are a confronter, then perhaps you need to figure out why you are so willing to hit a confrontation head-on. You may need to be more sensitive and considerate of others' feelings. If you really care about the individual and want an effective interaction, you need to carefully consider your response. Sometimes allowing a bit more time before dealing with an issue will be helpful to both you—the deliverer of the message—and the recipient. That gives the recipient time to self-reflect and calm down. The deliverer can thoughtfully consider a response and potentially gather some additional relevant data.

For most of us, we would prefer that conflict and difficult situations not be a part of our life. These difficult circumstances create anxiety and stress in us; however, it is unrealistic and counterproductive to mistakenly think we can avoid these situations. It fact, it is impossible. Funneling our energy into avoidance does not solve anything, and it can be very destructive in terms of relationships.

It is helpful to figure out where you fall on the conflict continuum. The continuum that ranges from "avoider" to "confronter" (see figure 2.1).

Are you the confronter—someone who embraces or even seeks out difficult and/or conflicting situations? Or are you an avoider—someone who avoids conflict or difficult situations at all costs? Most likely you fall somewhere close to one end or the other. Where you should be is somewhere in the reasonable middle.

You need to be aware of where you fall in the spectrum. First you need to realistically figure out where you are on the continuum. The second step is accepting where you are on the scale. Self-awareness and self-acceptance are key factors as you travel the road to self-improvement and personal and professional growth.

Before you can successfully engage in the principles of effective conversation, you need to understand your own tendencies. If you are a conflict

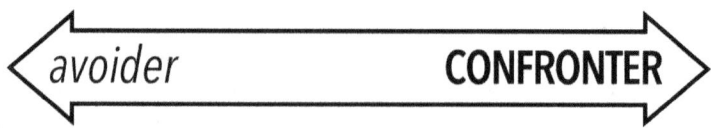

Figure 2.1. The Conflict Continuum. *Source*: Illustrated by Austin Wisler

avoider but will not admit that you are, you will likely not allow yourself to be impacted by the principles outlined in this book. If you are a conflict confronter but are not honest with yourself about it, you may think you already handle difficult situations correctly and do not need to change. Look around and you will see that most people can use some pointers on how to have better conversations.

WHY WE DON'T DEAL WITH THINGS

To deal with the behavior that manifests itself in making us want to avoid conflicting situations, it is helpful to look at the reasons we try to avoid confrontation. In general, it is because conflict is viewed as negative. Naturally we try to avoid negative things. The following are some of the specific explanations or excuses we use for avoiding the conversation:

- We do not know exactly what to say.
- We feel like there is no time to devote to the issue and dealing with it will take time away from more important tasks.
- We are afraid of being vulnerable, perhaps having to admit we were wrong.
- We fear that having the conversation will escalate the situation.
- We do not really care about or respect the person(s) involved.
- We believe it will be a waste of time and that nothing will change as a result of the conversation.
- We fear the unknown and wonder things like what will they say, how will they react, and what if they say or ask something I am unprepared to address or respond to?

Burt was a chronic conflict avoider and fell at the avoider end of the continuum. He hated conflict and avoided difficult situations, that is, until he confronted his fear. He still does not love it but is now much less apprehensive about confronting issues in an appropriate manner.

Burt's experiences and certain mentors and bosses had a positive impact on moving him more toward the middle of the continuum. He is still not as close to the middle as he feels he should be, but there has definitely been a shift in his thinking. He had mentors/supervisors/superiors that fell at various spots on the avoider/confronter continuum. Some were great at confronting situations. They pushed him to see the tremendous value in others and himself in tackling situations head-on. Some were closer to the other end of the spectrum and would often avoid or gloss over difficult situations. They would discount the severity in an effort to be positive and always think the best. This is not a bad quality, but it's not always effective when dealing with difficult circumstances.

The greatest impact on changing Burt's perspective and approach came from one boss in particular. His name was Walter. Walter fell at the confronter end of the spectrum. Several months after starting to work for Walter, he confronted Burt and said, "You just don't like conflict." He made the statement based on Burt's handling (or lack thereof) of a certain job performance situation Walter had been made aware of.

Walter was one of those individuals who welcomed a good confrontation/conflict. In fact, at times it felt like he sought out a good confrontation. He would fuel the fire, so to speak, with comments that would generate an emotionally charged response. He typically meant no harm by it. It was "sport" to him.

When he confronted Burt with the statement, "You just don't like conflict," Burt did not know how to respond and was caught off guard. He wanted to defensively and definitively answer that Walter was wrong. He knew his boss was not paying him a compliment. Burt also wondered if there was something wrong with not liking conflict. Obviously, Walter thought so.

After thinking about his comment for some time and after a bit of difficult self-reflection, Burt came to the conclusion that Walter was absolutely right. He not only disliked conflict, but also did everything he could to avoid it. It was a painful realization, something Burt was sure he knew about himself but never wanted to admit and certainly did not confront. Apparently he avoided that, too!

It bothered him to confront his own weakness, but he found comfort in knowing that most people do try to avoid conflict. In fact, enjoying conflict seems contrary to what most people strive for, which is less stress, less conflict, more happiness, and better and more satisfying relationships. He also took comfort in knowing that because he was willing to admit the conflict avoidance issue, he could now do something about it. He could work on his own leadership improvement, as well as enhancing his existing relationships.

The comment certainly impacted and affected him because it made him confront his own weakness. It got him thinking about the idea of confrontational situations, crucial conversations, and effective conversation principles for every conversation. Although the initial question from Walter was tough, in the end Burt was appreciative of the fact that it challenged him and made him a better leader.

The word *confrontation* conjures up many unpleasant thoughts. Although it may have the perception of being negative, try to think about it in terms of a challenge dealt with through conversation. Think about it in terms of developing and practicing an optimistic approach to the situation with the goal of achieving positive results. Most difficult and conflicting situations must be confronted to enhance productivity and promote healthy relationships.

WHY WE SHOULD DEAL WITH IT

There are many reasons for avoiding the conversation, but there are much better reasons not to avoid it. Research has shown that effective leadership and meaningful relationships are built on trust that is developed and enhanced through meaningful conversations. The downsides and dangers of ignoring a situation that should be dealt with are much greater than the potential downsides of dealing with the situation.

Some difficult situations work themselves out, but most will just get worse with time. Emotions and feelings may become exaggerated. The situation may be shared among others to garner support. Before you know it, the situation has escalated, intensified, and gotten out of hand.

In addition, if you do not deal with the situation in a timely manner, you run the risk of either party not remembering the facts of the situation. Think about it in terms of court trials. Trials that drag on are more difficult to adjudicate because the lapse of time creates a situation where the facts are fuzzy or forgotten.

There are three major reasons to deal with a difficult situation: (1) you care about people, especially the people you work with, supervise, and/or have a relationship with; (2) you care about your organization or business (if it is a work situation); and (3) you care about yourself.

Reason 1: You Care about People

No matter how tough the situation or how difficult the individual, dealing with it sends a strong signal to the individual. The message you send is that you care about and respect them. And simply put, you need to care. An effective leader cares about the people who are within their purview and scope. Caring about people is a crucial quality of good leaders. Caring about people is at the core of meaningful and authentic relationships.

In terms of the need to care in the workplace, studies show it is an important ingredient of satisfied and engaged employees. Satisfied and engaged employees are more productive. There is evidence to support the fact that people do not quit their job, they quit their boss.

In fact, according to a Gallup poll of more than one million U.S. workers, 75 percent of workers who voluntarily left their jobs did so because of their bosses. Research also shows that there are eight major reasons workers gave for quitting. Four of those top eight reasons could have been addressed through good conversations. The four of the top eight that involve conversation are poor communication (reason 2), not sharing information (reason 3), failure to listen (reason 5), and simply not caring about the individual (reason 8). These reasons are about the conversation, communication, and the relationship.[2]

It is important to care about turnover and losing good employees. The average price to replace an employee is $45,000 to $150,000, and it could be much more than that if it is an extremely valuable employee who has the potential to negatively impact your business in a big way. If you really do not care about people, then pretend and practice a caring attitude. If you continue to act like you care, it will eventually become part of your DNA.

You can change and control your behavior. Practice a simple thing, like saying hello and smiling to every individual you cross paths with. That practice will eventually become a habit, as will other "people-caring" gestures and behaviors you consistently practice.

Phillapa Lally, a health psychology researcher at University College London, and her team studied how long it takes to actually form a habit. The study examined the habits of ninety-six people during a twelve-week period. Each person chose one new habit for the twelve-week period. Each day the individuals reported on whether they did the chosen behavior. They also reported on how automatic the behavior felt.

The behaviors chosen varied in terms of difficulty, from things like drinking a bottle of water with lunch to running for fifteen minutes before dinner. At the end of the twelve weeks, the team analyzed the data to determine how long it took from the time a new behavior was started until it became automatic. The study revealed that, on average, it took about two months.

Obviously, how long it takes is dependent on the behavior, the person, and the circumstances. In the study, it took anywhere from 18 to 254 days (2 to 8 months). The study also found that missing the behavior a few times did not materially affect the habit formation process. The good news is that building better habits is not an all-or-nothing concept and you can take a good behavior and make it a habit. Practice caring about people so that it becomes a habit.

Reason 2: You Care about the Organization

If you care about the organization you are working for, you will also want to deal with the situation. The situation has the potential to affect the overall success of the organization. The conversation may reveal behavior that needs to be addressed and corrected.

Initially, it may seem that dealing with a situation is too time consuming. Dealing with it will pull you away from more important tasks, at least from your vantage point. In the end, not dealing with it at the appropriate time may cost you time and money.

Dealing with employee behavior (good or bad) in an appropriate manner is important. Year-end employee evaluations that are a listing of the things the employee failed at throughout the year are not effective. It is unfair to the employee if the annual evaluation meeting is the first time they are getting this feedback. Feedback, both negative and positive, that is given throughout the year is much more effective. Praise is much more meaningful if done immediately. Immediate praise reinforces more of the same behavior. Constructive criticism is more effective if done in a timely fashion. That way the individual can address the feedback and make changes while the incident is fresh in their minds.

The absence of information creates many issues. An employee may erroneously think they are not meeting expectations and act or react accordingly. Or, if an employee thinks they are exceeding expectations but in reality they are not even meeting them, that creates an entirely new set of issues. If the behavior is not addressed appropriately, others in the organization (who are most likely watching) may let the unaddressed behavior negatively impact their own actions and performance. The bottom line is that happy and engaged employees will positively affect an organization's bottom line.

Reason 3: You Care about Yourself

Even if you do not care about the people or the organization, you certainly care about yourself. Do it for yourself. It is unhealthy to carry around the uncomfortableness that comes from not dealing with a situation. Even if you do not think it is bothering you or think it is not on your mind, chances are it is there somewhere, even if only in your subconscious. Why chance that avoiding it may be causing you undue stress that you may or may not be aware of? Take care of the situation.

Even if the issue is only smoldering beneath the surface, it could reignite at any point. You may think that the "fire" is out or at least almost out, but it may be reignited with the smallest of sparks. Take care of it. You will feel better knowing that you did.

Timing Is Everything

Although the most important thing is that you deal with the situation and have the conversation, it is also important to carefully consider the timing of the conversation. Each situation needs to be assessed before deciding to deal with it immediately or waiting for a more appropriate time. Assess your emotional state and the state of the individual(s) involved.

Sometimes it is best to deal with the situation immediately, and sometimes it is best to wait. Do not procrastinate, but do not rush into it either. If you deal with it immediately, you run the risk of an emotional and potentially damaging response. If you wait too long, it creates a situation that is stressful for both parties. The other party might be wondering when the shoe will drop, and you may be wondering what will happen next.

A good balance between the two is where you should try to be. Unfortunately, we tend to handle each situation the same because of where we fall on the avoider/confronter continuum. Assess each situation and make adjustments so that each circumstance is approached in the right way and with the right timing. Make sure you analyze each situation and its unique factors before rushing in or waiting too long. Remember, timing is everything.

SUMMARY

Although there are more excuses for avoiding conflict and difficult conversations than there are reasons to deal with them, the benefits of dealing with these situations far outweigh the ramifications of not dealing with them. In fact, there really are no benefits to avoiding the situation. The negative consequences could be devastating. The potentially positive results are worth any risks you may believe exist by dealing with it.

So, step one is to decide that you need to deal with the situation. You will see that if you make this a practice, it will become more comfortable and more natural. Most likely it will never be easy, but it will become easier. Confrontational conversations and situations are never easy. They involve people, and people are not easy. The rest of this book is devoted to making sure the interaction is effective, meaningful, and positive.

CHAPTER 2 RECAP

- Figure out and acknowledge where you are on the avoider/confronter continuum.
- Realize you can improve your approach and behavior when it comes to confrontation.
- Accept that it is better to deal with difficult situations rather than avoid them.
- Realize that avoiding a difficult conversation can be costly.
- Make sure you consider the timing of dealing with the situation.
- Strive to have an authentic, honest, and heartfelt conversation. It is the best way to handle a conflict or difficult situation.

NOTES

1. Stephen M. R. Covey, *The Speed of Trust: The One Thing That Changes Everything* (New York: Free Press, 2006), 185.

2. Jennifer Robison, "Turning around Employee Turnover: Costly Churn Can Be Reduced if Managers Know What to Look for—and They Usually Don't," Gallup, May 8, 2008. Accessed July 18, 2019, https://news.gallup.com/businessjournal/106912/turning-around-your-turnover-problem.aspx; Marcel Schwantes, "Why Do Employees Really Quit Their Jobs? Research Says It Comes Down to These Top 8 Reasons," *INC*, September 21, 2017. Accessed July 18, 2019, https://www.inc.com/marcel-schwantes/why-are-your-employees-quitting-a-study-says-it-comes-down-to-any-of-these-6-reasons.html.

Chapter Three

Control Your Emotions

> Self-control is strength. Right thought is mastery. Calmness is power.
> —James Allen

Those who are unable to manage their emotions are often ill-prepared to deal with conflict. It is difficult and sometimes impossible to have a meaningful and effective conversation if emotions are not in check. Oftentimes emotions drive the conversation and are not aligned with a rational approach. Understanding emotions and, in particular, your emotional makeup and triggers is the first step to managing your emotions. Once you understand what is driving your emotions you can then practice behaviors that help you effectively manage them.

UNDERSTANDING EMOTIONS

Psychology once assumed that most emotions fell within the following six universal and distinct categories of emotions:

1. happiness
2. sadness
3. anger
4. surprise
5. fear
6. disgust

A more recent study from the Greater Good Science Center, as reported by faculty director Dacher Keltner, suggests that there are more than twenty-seven distinct emotions and that they are intimately connected with one another.[1] That means that emotional experiences and responses are much more complex and nuanced than originally thought. This study and its findings raise the level of importance of discussing emotions relative to challenging conversations.

It is natural for our emotions to drive our behavior. Think about how you act and react to different circumstances. It is typically an emotionally driven response. We do not usually take the time to figure out what a rational response should be. We may blurt out the response and then think about it later. We need to resist being controlled by our emotions.

Emotions are not fixed facts. Emotions are flexible and can be changed. Emotions are driven by how you are interpreting a story or situation. It is your perception of what is happening—your perception as to why a person did what they did. Your emotions are driven purely by your perspective and what you think is going on. Do you really know what someone else is thinking? Do you know enough about the other person to know why they may have acted the way they did? Chances are you do not. We cannot know the thoughts, background, current situation, and everything that is going on in someone else's mind. We see it through our lens, our filter.

Road rage seems to be an ever-increasing issue. When you see the reckless or stupid behavior of someone behind the wheel of a vehicle, do you ever wonder what they might be going through at the present time? Perhaps they have just received terrible news, or perhaps they are racing to the hospital in an emergency situation. It does not excuse the behavior, but it does help us manage our own emotions and behavior if we put ourselves in someone else's shoes. If you attempt to see the picture in their head and then let it go, you will be less stressed. Stress is not good. Let go of the anger—do it for yourself, if for no other reason.

Cognitive behavioral therapy is a short-term form of psychotherapy directed at present issues. It is based on the idea that the way an individual thinks and feels affects the way he or she behaves. The goal of the therapy is to change an individual's thought patterns in order to change their response to difficult situations. The idea is that you can change the way you see something so that your behavior and emotional response is different.

According to an article in *Psychology Today*, positive psychology is a method of therapy similar to cognitive behavioral therapy. Positive psychology promotes ways that you can change your emotional responses. By changing the story that we see in our heads, we can change the emotions. If you tell yourself a different story, you will automatically generate a different emotion and emotional response. Positive psychology also suggests that by changing your behavior, you change your emotions. You can give your emotions a jumpstart by playing the part even if you are not feeling it. Behave differently and people will respond differently. For instance, if you play the calm one in a conflict, the opponent's response often makes it increasingly easy for you to continue to play the calm one.[2]

Trying to change your emotions and be the calm one in a volatile situation is contrary to the way we automatically react. Many parents teach their children to stand up for themselves. They are taught to fight back when confronted with aggression. Not all parents fall into that group. Some parents teach their children to look the other way, to resist the instinct to fight back based on certain religious beliefs. We all have been affected by our upbringing, and our experiences and behaviors reflect that background.

Customer service representative is certainly a position that lends itself to someone who can remain calm given any circumstance. Any industry—especially the service industry—where customers are part of the equation requires staff who are able to manage their emotions even in the most difficult circumstances.

Back in the day, when Sears was a powerhouse in the retail space, staff on the sales floor were taught that the "customer is always right." By starting with that premise, it set a standard for the behavior Sears expected from its sales force. Regardless of how ridiculous a customer's complaint, request, or reason for returning an item, the customer was given the benefit of the doubt. That philosophy set the tone for employees. If you had a short temper and a combative personality, you were quickly encouraged to find other employment.

The business manager in a school district must be someone who can control their emotions. Soon after the property tax bills are distributed there is no shortage of calls from angry and disgruntled taxpayers. Being able to remain calm and find ways to de-escalate the situation become important skills of the position. Expressing empathy, remaining calm, and offering assistance and suggestions for funneling the taxpayer's anger are critical components of having an effective conversation. There is no time to think or plan your particular message; therefore, remaining calm and listening are the most important strategies. Typically, a calm and empathetic approach de-escalates the situation, and although the individual may not be happy, they oftentimes feel that they have been heard and understood.

The wrong thing to do as a business manager is to engage in an argument, trying to prove that the taxpayer is wrong and that you are not receptive to their "story." Trying to rationalize with an angry, disgruntled taxpayer does not work. It is wrong to enter the conversation with your own anger about the fact that you have to take the call—which may have been the tenth difficult phone call of the day. It is ineffective to try to talk over them by explaining that the tax rate is approved by the board of school directors and if they have an issue they should attend a board meeting. Additionally, if they do not pay the tax bill, it will be sent to the delinquent tax collector and they will have additional fees, interest, and penalties. That response creates a firestorm of shouting back and forth. It is not an effective approach. Yet, sometimes it is used to try to convey a sense of control and authority, and a way to insist that they see things your way. It does not work and you end up being stressed and upset, and the taxpayer is even angrier than when they first called. Don't do it. Let them vent, listen to their concerns, express your understanding of their situation, and then offer any help or suggestions you may have.

WHY IT IS IMPORTANT TO CONTROL YOUR EMOTIONS

An emotional response can be authentic and honest, but it can be very damaging as well. When emotions are running wild you may say something that is inappropriate, unprofessional, and hurtful. Once the words have been spoken it is impossible to pull them back. The damage has been done, and repairing the damage may take a great deal of time and energy—and may not even be possible. During those times of high emotion, it may feel good to let it out, to express what you are feeling. The release may feel good at the time until you look at the collateral damage. You may ruin the relationship over something that seemed big at the time but in the grand scheme of things was not worth the consequences.

In the workplace, an emotional response can be damaging to you as a leader. It is not good to exhibit anger or rage in a professional setting. Decisions should be made on the basis of rational thinking and not just an emotional response. Emotions are certainly a core part of most decisions, but they should not be the driving force. People are watching your leadership style, and if they detect it is driven by emotion, they will adjust their behavior accordingly.

An effective leader and a well-adjusted individual understands their own emotions. What are your red flags? What are the words or phrases that really set you off? What are the behaviors that really annoy you? A great interview question for a job applicant is, "What is it that you cannot tolerate in an office environment?" It really tries to get at whether the candidate understands themselves and knows what "annoyance triggers" they have. The response can give insight into whether they will fit in your company's culture. A response of, "It really drives me crazy when people are not serious about their work and are not focused on their responsibilities," indicates that someone may not fit into and/or be happy in a more flexible, loose work environment.

If you are aware of your own "annoyance triggers" you are much more likely to be able to control them. In the heat of a conversation, if someone says or does something that you know is a hot-button issue for you, you can step back and not let that trigger derail the entire conversation. The other individual is likely unaware that they have set off the trigger.

THE ANGER DANGER ZONE

Rage and anger are two emotions that are not going anywhere anytime soon. A 2016 survey by Esquire/NBC found that although there were differences among the groups they surveyed, the overall presence of rage is clear. In fact, of the more than 3,000 American adults included in the survey, about half were angrier today than they were a year ago.[3] We need to get control of our anger.

In a challenging conversation, your emotions must be properly managed. It often happens in the heat of the moment. Driven by emotion, you end up ruining a relationship, escalating a situation, or making it impossible to move toward resolution. Once something is said, it is impossible to hit the erase button. We know it, but we still fall into the trap. We are so upset or angry we just blurt it out. It feels good in the moment. We feel a sense of victory in letting the person know, in no uncertain terms, how we feel; however, once we step back and our emotions settle a bit, we see that there is collateral damage. Now we do not feel as good and are left to pick up the pieces.

CONTROLLING YOUR EMOTIONS

There are ways you can control your emotions. First you have to be aware of them. Acknowledge how you feel. Then agree that you have a choice. You can choose to give in to the emotion or choose to change it. Choosing not to give in to an emotion, for example, anger, is not a weakness. Sometimes we believe that showing anger is an indication to others that we are tough, that we have the upper hand, that we are right. Suppressing the anger or, better yet, changing the anger to a more positive emotion is not a sign of weakness.

Anger is probably the most common emotion associated with difficult and challenging situations. Fighting is typically associated with anger. When we are angry, we fight. It is sort of a natural pairing. Fighting is a symbol of strength, so therefore we correlate anger with strength. On the contrary, not giving in to anger takes great strength. A strong, effective leader will not be controlled by emotions. Decisions based on emotion are typically flawed decisions.

If you are not able to suppress the undesirable emotion on your own, there are other ways to deal with it. Find a trusted friend who can help you. They may be able to talk you through your emotions. They may see the situation in a different way, which will be helpful. In many cases, you will work yourself through it as you relay the situation to another individual.

Sometimes it may be as simple as just walking away from the situation. Change your focus. Take a deep breath, and get involved in something else.

A distraction may be all you need to get control of your emotions and let them go.

Another strategy is to thoughtfully consider how the other person is seeing things. Find the "picture" in their head. What is it that may be causing them to see things differently than you do? It's not necessarily right or wrong, it's just different. Extend to them the benefit of the doubt. You may have no idea what life circumstances they are dealing with.

It may be helpful to write down your thoughts. Writing may help you sort out your thoughts. It forces you to carefully think about the situation and the individual(s) involved. Write down a proposed response. Think about a follow-up conversation. What is the desired outcome of that conversation? Think about the message and the words you want to use. Obviously at the point that you are writing these thoughts down it is a one-sided conversation. Your message will have to be adjusted based on the response. There is tremendous value in writing down what you plan to say. The very fact that you are writing down your message helps you gain control of your emotions.

Writing down your message will assist you when you have the actual conversation. Although you will not be following the script word for word, the fact that you wrote it down will assist you tremendously when you actually have the conversation. Research shows that writing something down creates a much greater chance of recall at a later date. According to an article by Mark Murphy on Forbes.com, study after study shows that you remember things better if you write them down. When interviewers took notes about the interviewee, they were able to recall 23 percent more of the interviewee's responses than the interviewers who did not take notes. Writing not only helps you remember, but also makes your mind more efficient because you are focusing on the things that really matter—the important details.[4]

Murphy also reports on the "generation effect," identified by neuropsychologists. It basically says individuals demonstrate a greater memory for things they have generated themselves than things that have been generated by someone else and they only read. When you write it down (generate it), you create a picture in your head that assists you in the recall process.

Another helpful tip is to ask a close, trusted friend or colleague to critique your message. Get their feedback and have them assess the effectiveness and appropriateness of your message. Having the message evaluated through another set of eyes is never a bad thing. Even if you never get a chance to deliver your message, the exercise of writing down your thoughts is invaluable.

To work toward a successful outcome, you will need to have your emotions in check. You cannot control someone else's emotions, but you can control your own. You need to model the appropriate behavior.

The idea that controlling your emotions is a sign of great strength is an important point. We tend to believe that we have the upper hand when we exhibit the most anger and are the loudest and the most agitated. The notion that whoever has the greatest anger is the most important is ridiculous. Yet, we model and behave the wrong way all the time. As we interact with others, we try to "one-up" our level of anger or frustration—for example, "Yes, I know that you are angry about that, but wait until you hear what happened to me, I have reason to be even angrier than you."

The truth is, you control the situation when you control your emotions. You have the upper hand when your emotions are in check and properly managed.

OTHER EMOTIONS

Although we've mostly talked about anger, we need to be aware of other emotions that may surface. We focus on anger because it tends to be the most prevalent in difficult circumstances and confrontations. Exhibiting laughter, happiness, or insincerity during a serious interaction can be just as damaging as an anger-infused interaction. Laughter and insincerity will be interpreted as you not taking the circumstances seriously. The other party will assume you are dismissing or discounting their feelings. Figuratively speaking, it is a slap in the face.

Fear is another emotion that may show up. If you are in a leadership role, reflecting fear during a situation will most likely compromise your leadership ability. It will be viewed as weakness and uncertainty. Exhibiting some level of confidence even in tenuous, unknown situations can be an asset. Being confident in these situations does not mean you cannot show vulnerability and be caring. It does not mean you get to be arrogant. Strive for a healthy balance between being fearful and overconfident or arrogant.

There is a great quote by Fedor Emelianenko, Ukrainian-born Russian heavyweight mixed martial artist, that illustrates this point:

> A fighter, a real strong fighter, should always look dignified and calm, and I believe that any expression of aggression is an expression of weakness. A strong person will not be nervous and will not express aggression towards his opponent. He will be confident in his abilities and his training; then he will face the fight calm and balanced. [5]

This quote does a great job of summarizing what it means to be in control of your emotions and the tremendously positive impact you can have by exhibiting a calm and balanced approach.

Showing disgust during a conversation can also be detrimental to a meaningful conversation. It can be seen as judgmental—that you have already decided how you feel about a circumstance even though you have not heard the other party out. This is especially true if the individual is offering a heartfelt acknowledgment that they did something wrong. Showing disgust is not appropriate.

SUMMARY

The bottom line is that you need to be aware of your emotional state and take steps to reflect the appropriate type and level of emotion during an interaction. Emotions are not bad, they just need to be properly managed.

We need emotions. Emotions can be helpful in assisting in the development of a successful outcome. Using such emotions as empathy, concern, and openness can be a real asset in authentic conversations. Not showing any emotion can be just as damaging as showing the wrong emotion. The appropriate emotion and the right amount of that emotion at the right time is a crucial part of the formula for having a successful interaction.

CHAPTER 3 RECAP

- Understand your emotions and your triggers.
- Control your emotions, as you cannot control someone else's.
- Remember that an emotional response can get you into trouble.
- Think about your response prior to responding.
- Beware of anger; fighting back is not a symbol of strength.
- Know when to walk away from the situation.
- It is not bad to show controlled emotion, but do not be driven by emotions alone.
- There are ways to get control of your emotions. Seek the advice of a colleague or friend. Step away for a period of time. Consider how the other party is viewing the situation. Put yourself in their shoes. Write down your feelings and a proposed response, and then delete it or throw it away.

NOTES

1. Yasmin Anwar, "How Many Different Human Emotions Are There," *Greater Good Magazine*, September 8, 2017. Accessed July 18, 2019, https://greatergood.berkeley.edu/article/item/how_many_different_human_emotions_are_there.

2. Jeremy E. Sherman, "Total Control vs. No Control Theory of Emotions: Can You Control Your Emotions or Not?" *Psychology Today*, June 13, 2010. Accessed July 18, 2019, https://www.psychologytoday.com/us/blog/ambigamy/201006/total-control-vs-no-control-theory-emotions-can-you-control-your-emotions-or.

3. Rabbi David Wolpe, "Why Americans Are so Angry about Everything," *Time*, January 5, 2016. Accessed July 18, 2019, https://time.com/4166326/why-americans-are-so-angry-about-everything/.

4. Mark Murphy, "Neuroscience Explains Why You Need to Write Down Your Goals if You Actually Want to Achieve Them," *Forbes*, April 15, 2018. Accessed June 24, 2019, https://www.forbes.com/sites/markmurphy/2018/04/15/neuroscience-explains-why-you-need-to-write-down-your-goals-if-you-actually-want-to-achieve-them/.

5. Fedor Emelianenko, quoted in, "Fedor Emelianenko Quotes," BrainyQuote, n.d. Accessed July 19, 2019, https://www.brainyquote.com/authors/fedor_emelianenko.

Chapter Four

Create Safe Space

> I have learned that people will forget what you said, people will forget what you did, but people will never forget how you made them feel.
>
> —Maya Angelou

What is safe space? How can you create safe space? What makes a place "safe"? Is safe space the same for everyone? What are the benefits of safe space in terms of the conversation? These are great questions that need to be considered prior to engaging in a conversation. Safe space allows people to share their feelings in a nonthreatening environment. Safe space will increase the possibility that you will have a meaningful conversation with a positive and concrete outcome. In the absence of safe space, the conversation may just be an exercise in futility and a big waste of time.

The first step is to understand and acknowledge the importance of safety in a conversation. You must genuinely make an effort to create that safe space. Going through the motions to create safe space will not work. It must be an authentic attempt, otherwise it may actually work against what you are trying to accomplish.

Think about a time that you were involved in a conversation and you felt comfortable sharing. Sometimes you feel it right away when you meet someone. What is it that they exude that makes you feel safe? It is the feeling that they are genuinely interested in you. It is the way they listen, the questions they ask, and their body language, radiating a feeling of comfortableness. In a way, they have created a space that is safe and comfortable so that you feel free to share and converse.

DEFINING "SAFE" AND "SAFE SPACE"

According to *Merriam-Webster*, safe is defined as "free from harm or risk, secure from threat of danger, harm, or loss." Simply put, safe can be defined as free from harm or hurt. The harm or hurt might be physical or emotional. In many cases, emotional hurt can be more devastating than physical harm. Physical healing oftentimes happens quicker than emotional healing.

According to *Merriam-Webster*, safe space is defined as a "place intended to be free of bias, conflict, criticism, or potentially threatening actions, ideas, or conversations." The word *free* shows up in this definition as well. The idea is that hurtful comments and threatening actions are absent in this space.

According to FosteringPerspectives.org, one emotion we often feel, without consciously knowing it, is the feeling of safety.[1] Feeling safe is not something we discuss often. For example, when a friend asks, "How are you?" you typically do not respond by telling them that you feel safe. Yet, when you think about it, most of us would say we feel safe on a fairly regular basis.

WHEN WE FEEL UNSAFE

Think about a time when you did not feel safe. It might have been during a terrible storm, or when you got separated from friends or family in a crowd, or perhaps when you were walking down a dark street or alley alone. What emotions were you experiencing at that time? It is likely that several emotions were competing for your attention during that traumatic experience. You may have been scared and anxious. Your heart was most likely racing and your mind spinning trying to figure out what might happen next and what you should do. Understandably, you may have felt panic based on the fact that you were not in control of your body and mind's reaction. The point is, when you are afraid, you are not in a position to make good decisions. When you do not feel safe, you are not in a good place to have a meaningful and rational conversation.

SAFE IS NOT THE SAME FOR EVERYONE

Safe is a relative term. What might be considered safe for one person might not be safe in the eyes of someone else. Finding that safe zone is unique and personal to each person. Try to figure out what will make it safe for the person you are talking to. Sometimes it is as simple as stating that you want them to feel safe and be able to share freely during the conversation. Follow up that statement with a few questions. How can I create a space that will feel safe to you? Are there specific things that I can do or say to assure you that I want the space to be safe? Would it be helpful to have someone else here with you?

They will appreciate the fact that you care enough about them to make the effort. And you should care about them. Making them feel uncomfortable and afraid is not an effective way to deal with a difficult situation. It may make you feel superior, but in the end it is not beneficial in motivating the other party, caring for another person, or helping an individual improve. It is not conducive to a good conversation.

WHY CREATE SAFE SPACE?

Having the conversation in a safe space enhances the possibility of an authentic and meaningful exchange of information. Creating that safe space helps you get to the root of the problem. If the space is not safe, the conversation and meeting are likely to be ineffective. If true feelings are not shared, people will most likely leave the meeting without a resolution and with a feeling of unsatisfaction.

Trust is an important part of a creating a safe space. If you do not already have a trusting relationship with this individual, creating a trusting environment in an immediate manner will be difficult, if not impossible; however, if you want individuals to share freely, you will need to do your best to create a certain level of trust. The other party will need to be assured that the information will be kept confidential and that there will be no judgment in terms of what will be shared. As the initiator of the conversation, it is your responsibility to do your best to create the safe space. As host of the conversation, you may already feel safe because of your position. Regardless of whether the other party is interested in creating a safe space, as the initiator it is your responsibility to put forth the effort.

SAFE SPACE IN A DOCTOR'S OFFICE

Think about the importance of creating a safe space in a doctor's office. It might be a medical doctor, a dentist, or a psychiatrist. The patient needs to be able to express feelings, thoughts, background, prior conditions, current status, and other important factors. Without that sharing, there is a chance the treatment will be less effective or even ineffective. The doctor will have to fill in the blanks when information is withheld. There is a greater chance that there will be an improper diagnosis followed by an inappropriate treatment plan.

It is no different in a personal or professional conversational setting. Each party must know that they can share their honest thoughts and feelings if the intent is to reach a conclusion or an effective plan of action as a result of the conversation.

CREATING SAFE SPACE

What are some things that can be done to create safe space? There are four major things you can do to create a safe space in a face-to-face conversational situation. These four things create the safe space square. Paying attention to and addressing these four factors will improve the chances of a great conversation (see figure 4.1).

The Relationship

At the base of the square is the relationship. This is the most important factor in creating a safe space. If an authentic relationship already exists, you are one step ahead. If it is a meaningful and trusting relationship that has existed for some time, you will likely have to exert little effort to create that safe space. Your past interactions and history have already been established and will automatically create a sense of trust and safety.

There are many levels of a relationship that exist. The deeper the level, the less you will have to worry about the other factors (e.g., words, environment, body language). Shallower relationships will require that you pay close attention to the other factors. If no real relationship exists, you will need to spend extra time and expend extra effort making sure that the other factors are adequately addressed.

The Words

The second most important factor in the safe space square is the words. The words you use will matter. Be careful in your choice of words. Your words can be instrumental in creating a safe space. Use words of comfort and understanding—words that reflect that you truly care. Do not rush into the reason for and purpose of the intended conversation. Take a few minutes to create and show a personal interest in the other person. That means you should ask such questions as, "How are you doing?" "What are you working on?" and/or "Did you have a good weekend?" The type and nature of the questions and how in-depth you go will depend on the individual and the situation at hand. You need to determine the appropriateness of the questions based on your assessment of the situation and the person involved. This opening part of the conversation must be authentic; you need to show a genuine interest in and care for them. It will be different for each situation based on the level of relationship that already exists.

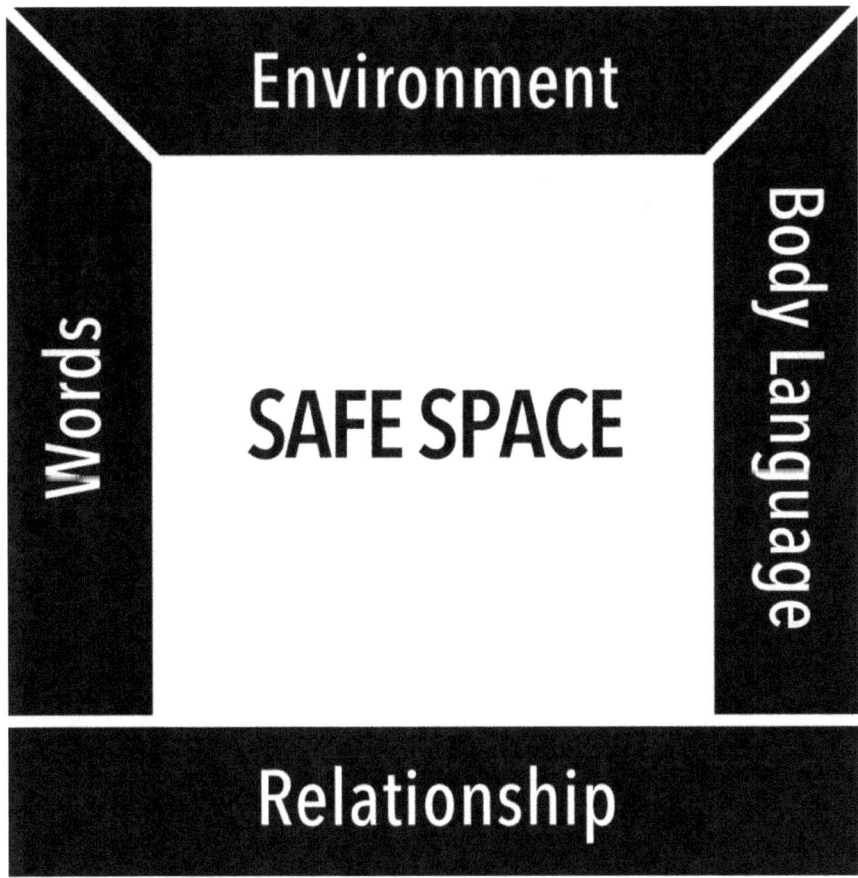

Figure 4.1. The Safe Space Square. *Source*: Illustrated by Austin Wisler

The Environment

Creating safe space requires attention to what can be called the environment. It is the physical location and timing of the meeting. If you are the initiator of the conversation, go to the other party. Hold the meeting in their space on their turf. Chances are they will feel safer in their own space. Absent that, find a space that is safer than your office. Your office may be perceived as the least safe space. The minute someone is told they need to stop and see the boss in their office, it immediately conjures up feelings of fear, defensiveness, and many other negative thoughts.

Make it a comfortable setting. Again, it always depends on the situation and the person involved. Every conversation is unique and may dictate a different setting. It would be an unusual situation that the appropriate setting is you sitting behind your desk, especially if you are in a position of authority. Sitting behind a desk makes you an imposing figure. The unspoken message is, "I am the boss and I have something to say—you will listen and obey."

More often than not, sitting at a small, round conference table or in an informal seating arrangement is more conducive to creating a safe space. The attempt is to even the playing field, to be on the same level as the other party.

Another factor in creating an overall safe environment is the timing of the conversation. As they say, "Timing is everything." Be sensitive to the time during which the meeting is scheduled. Depending on the circumstances, you may want to give the other person some notice of the meeting, or, in some cases, it may be more appropriate to just stop by and begin the conversation without any notice at all. Again, you will need to assess the situation based on the circumstances and the individual(s) involved.

Sometimes, if too much time lapses, the situation is exacerbated, and it creates unnecessary stress for the impacted individuals. If you do not have the necessary time to effectively deal with the entire situation, you may be able to reassure the individual(s) by indicating what the future conversation will be about. Share the topic and give them a glimpse of what you want to talk about to try to ease their minds.

Body Language

Use body language that is invitational rather than confrontational. Oftentimes, your body language speaks louder than your words. The following body language is considered confrontational and deters rich conversation:

- Leaning in close and crossing personal boundaries of space
- Displaying abrupt, aggressive gestures and other intimidating behavior
- Clenching your fist
- Shaking your head
- Rolling your eyes
- Making eye contact for an extended period of time, staring them down
- Placing hands on hips
- Crossing arms

On the other hand, there is body language that is inviting and open, for instance,

- Greeting with a firm handshake
- Maintaining a posture and body position that shows you are relaxed—back straight but not rigid, shoulders relaxed
- Leaning in slightly toward the person

- Aligning your body with the other person
- Mirroring the other person's facial expressions
- Maintaining good eye contact and avoiding staring or blinking too much
- Staying engaged in the conversation and taking notes to show you are actively listening
- Speaking slowly and clearly

Be aware of how you are coming across. Be deliberate about your body language. It may be necessary to overemphasize the invitational body language, even if it feels uncomfortable.

THE IMPORTANCE OF SAFE SPACE

Look at the medical profession in terms of safe space. There has been a change in the kind of space that is provided by doctors to patients. Years ago, the doctor was viewed as an authoritative figure who was rarely questioned. It was intimidating to talk with the doctor, who typically sat behind his desk in his office to deliver a medical diagnosis and the medical plan. In most cases, the approach was less than warm and fuzzy.

Doctors are now schooled in making the patient feel comfortable. They meet the patient on their level and truly listen to them. Now it is rare to see the inside of the doctor's actual office. The doctor meets with you in the examination room, sitting down next to you, at your level, to discuss what is going on. Their behaviors reflect a general interest in what you are saying as they probe for what you are feeling and experiencing. This is a much more comfortable environment. This is not to say that all doctors in the past took the authoritarian approach or that all doctors are now offering a comfortable environment. It is merely used to contrast and compare based on what many patients have experienced.

Another instance where it is important to create safe space is in an interview situation. Interviews can certainly be viewed as important conversations. Hiring appropriate and productive staff is crucial to the success of any organization. Hiring the right people and putting together an effective team of people is difficult but important.

You review a résumé, spend an hour or two in conversation with the individual, make a few reference checks, and then hire the person, hoping you made the right decision. What can you put in place to ensure that you are making the right decision? The concepts and benefits of safe space should be factored into an effective interview process.

One of the primary goals of the interview is to get to know the person you are interviewing. You want to understand who they are, what motivates them, what skills they have, and if they are the right fit for the organization and the position. You want to make sure that the person you saw in the interview is the same person who shows up after you hire them. In the interview, you do not just want to see the person they are presenting themselves to be. They are portraying themselves in the most positive light, in a way they think will get them the job. They may be creating an image of themselves that does not reflect who they really are. Many candidates prepare for the interview by reviewing the most common interview questions and Googling the "correct" responses, the ones they think employers want to hear. In an interview situation, how can you make sure you are getting to know the "real" person?

There is no surefire way to make sure you are getting to know the real person you are interviewing, but creating a space where the interviewee is comfortable can improve your chances of seeing the "real" person. If you make the candidate feel comfortable, they are more likely to share and exhibit who they really are.

How can you make a candidate feel comfortable in an interview situation? It is about creating that safe space through the interview environment, the words you use, and your body language.

Find a comfortable place for the interview. Sit around a table or find another comfortable seating arrangement. One effective way to meet a candidate and make them feel comfortable is to meet them for coffee in a public setting or perhaps in a private reception-type area where there are comfortable chairs and pleasant surroundings. Meet with them on their level, not behind your desk.

In terms of the words you use, try to start a brief conversation with them prior to jumping into the interview questions. Do your best to connect with them on an appropriate and somewhat personal basis. Ask them questions prior to the interview that invite sharing. Offer some limited sharing of your own. Look for any connection you may have with them. Find a way to help them relax, and show them that you are truly interested in them. Make sure the interview questions are geared toward getting at who they really are.

According to Anthony Hughes, a recruitment veteran of eighteen-plus years and cofounder of Coburg Banks, there are several interview questions that get at a candidate's true personality. The following are some examples that can be very effective. In the article, Hughes also offers some tips on what to look for in the responses to these questions.

- How would your best friend describe you?
- What do you do to get "in the zone?"
- If you could, what animal would you be and why?
- What are your pet peeves?
- What book do you think every person in this type of position should read?[2]

Use these types of questions to determine who the real person is. Questions like the one about what animal they would be may generate some laughter and make great strides in creating a more comfortable and relaxed environment, resulting in positive outcomes. Traditional interview questions deal more with their technical ability and capability for the job, as well as their experience.

In terms of body language, make sure you greet the interviewee with a firm handshake. Make sure you make the appropriate amount of eye contact and show genuine interest in what they are saying by taking notes. Ask follow-up questions to the scripted interview questions to see if there is consistency in their answers.

What you are really attempting to do is to get them to let their guard down. You want to see their true self. Getting the right person is important for the organization, but it is equally important for the individual. Finding the right fit is crucial for both. An individual in the wrong job will not be happy. Employees spend more time at work than any other place, so it is important that they be happy and not miserable. Additionally, in terms of the organization, the wrong person can cost a lot of time and money. It is expensive and time consuming to rectify a bad hire. It is better to do everything in your power to hire the right person. Creating safe space in an interview situation can improve your chances of doing just that.

SUMMARY

At the core of creating safe space is trust. You are trying to create a trusting environment. A certain level of trust is key to a meaningful conversation; however, creating that trusting and safe space has become increasingly difficult. Research shows that there has been an incredible erosion of overall trust since the 1960s. People are less trusting of their coworkers, their bosses, and the organizations they work for.

According to a 2018 article entitled "Trust Is Collapsing in America," written by Uri Friedman and published in the *Atlantic*, only 33 percent of Americans trust that their government will do what is right. This is down fourteen points from just one year ago. Trust in business and nongovernmental organizations decreased by ten and nine points, respectively, in just a one-year period. The communications marketing firm Edelman, the firm that conducted the survey, has been surveying the level of trust in various institutions for the past eighteen years and has never recorded such a steep decrease in trust from respondents in the United States.[3]

It is important to be aware of what is going on around us. The decline in overall trust is a major concern and needs to be factored in when you are attempting to create that safe, comfortable, and trusting environment. This means it will be harder and harder to put things in place that will create that safe space and build that trust.

Although trust is built throughout time, in most difficult conversation situations, you do not have the luxury of having built that trust with the individual; therefore, it is essential that you work on the other three factors (environment, words, and body language) to create a sense of safe and trusting space. By working on those factors, you will improve the chance that the person will trust you and be able to share in a safe and comfortable space.

CHAPTER 4 RECAP

- A safe space is one in which individuals feel free from bias, conflict, potentially threatening actions, and judgment. A safe space is a place where there is a sense of trust that issues can be shared without fear.
- Safe space is crucial in having a meaningful conversation, especially in dealing with a difficult situation.
- It is easier to create that safe space if there is an existing positive relationship with the individual involved in the situation.
- An important component of creating that safe space is through the words we use.
- Body language can enhance or deter the creation of that safe space.
- The environment (physical location and timing of the meeting) for the conversation is an important part of creating safe space.
- The relationship, environment, words, and body language work together to create the optimal safe space for those difficult conversations.

NOTES

1. Jeanne Preisler, "Being Safe vs. Feeling Safe," *Fostering Perspectives*, May 2013. Accessed June 24, 2019, http://fosteringperspectives.org/fpv17n2/psychological-safety.html.

2. Anthony Hughes, "Eleven Interview Questions That Will Reveal Your Candidate's True Personality," Coburg Banks, n.d. Accessed June 24, 2019, https://www.coburgbanks.co.uk/blog/assessing-applicants/11-interview-questions-that-will-reveal-your-candidates-true-personality/.

3. Uri Friedman, "Trust Is Collapsing in America," *Atlantic*, January 21, 2018. Accessed June 24, 2019, https://www.theatlantic.com/international/archive/2018/01/trust-trump-america-world/550964/.

Chapter Five

Speak from the Heart

A good head and a good heart are always a formidable combination.
—Nelson Mandela

Speaking from the heart is really about effective communication. What is at the core of successful communication? There are three core beliefs that are related and intertwined, and at the heart of valued and effective communication:

1. Showing concern for others
2. Maintaining a sense of humility
3. Keeping an attitude of service above self

It is almost impossible to communicate effectively and engage in a rich conversation without these three things. Communication involves caring for the individual you are talking to. If you do not really care about the person, you will just be going through the motions. You need to care, especially if it is an employee, a colleague, a family member, or a friend.

A sense of humility shows that you do not have all the answers. This is particularly important if it is a conversation with an employee you supervise. But it is also important in every conversation. No one likes the "know-it-all." You do not know it all. Quite frankly, there is almost always something that can be learned from every conversation. Approach the conversation with a sense of humility. Approach the conversation with the wonder of what you might be able to learn. Anticipate that perhaps the other person may have something to offer. What they have to offer might be even better than what you bring to the table.

A "service above self" approach shows the other person it is not all about you. Just like no one likes the know-it-all, no one likes the self-absorbed person either. The idea is that you are interested in them and a successful outcome from the conversation. In this case, success is defined as the place where both sides have benefited from the conversation. Success is not leaving the conversation feeling like you were victorious.

THE HEART AND THE BRAIN

The heart is the traditional symbol for love; therefore, speaking from the heart means you speak out of care and concern for the individual. You have a desire to help the person. It implies that you care for the person and find value in them. It means that as you are speaking, you are doing so with some measure of positive feeling. The feelings you display might be empathy, joy, interest, sincerity, or gratitude.

Speaking from the heart does not mean you disengage the brain. You still need to be smart about the approach you take. Express appropriate feelings at the appropriate time. People involved in difficult conversations are typically emotional. Thus, speaking strictly from the intellect does not work. Individuals are usually more emotional and less rational. A challenging conversation requires a more emotional, from-the-heart approach.

There are plenty of examples of speaking strictly from the brain. So many of our approaches deal with the facts of the case, and we fail to add the human element. People connect better when there is an emotional tie-in. How many times have you heard someone say, "I just need to give them a piece of my mind"? It happens all the time. Some people say that but then just let it go. Plenty of other people say that and then act on it.

For instance, a person does something that you do not think is right, and you immediately call them out on it. How many times have you seen that approach be effective? You approach someone and call them out for something they did that you felt was wrong. You respond out of emotion even though you think you are "giving them a piece of your mind." In most cases, the message is not received well. In fact, the receiver typically gets angry and defensive. That "conversation" travels to the receiver's friends and does not make for good relationship building, especially between the message deliverer and the receiver.

In fact, the only person who has any chance of feeling better from the interaction is the message deliverer. Perhaps they have a sense of satisfaction that they spoke their mind. Has it really helped anything? Chances are the message was not received in a way that will cause that individual to make any positive change. In fact, if given the opportunity to do it again in front of the person, they likely would. It would be done out of spite.

Think about that before you speak your mind next time. Is it really an effective way of communicating? If you really feel strongly about the action of the other person, you should approach them in a kinder, gentler way with a genuine attitude of concern for them. Try to understand why they acted the way they did. They may have no idea that their action was interpreted the way it was.

Working together, the brain and the heart make a powerful team. Speaking from the heart means you are using emotional intelligence concepts. In the book *Emotional Intelligence* by Daniel Goleman, he talks about the importance of the softer skills. He compares the effectiveness of emotional intelligence (EI) versus the more traditional measure of success, the intelligence quotient (IQ). Goleman describes a specific profile of competencies that range across four different areas of personal ability.

1. self-awareness
2. self-management
3. empathy and social awareness
4. relationship management[1]

An April 11, 2017 posting on the Key Step Media website summarizes the crucial competencies of emotional intelligence (often referred to as EI or EQ). The summary includes the following definition of emotional intelligence: "EI is the capacity to recognize our own feelings and those of others, and to manage emotions effectively in ourselves and our relationships."[2]

Research carried out by the Carnegie Institute of Technology shows that 85 percent of your financial success is due to skills in what they called "human engineering." Human engineering can be described as your personality and your ability to communicate, negotiate, and lead. Only 15 percent is due to technical knowledge.[3] Additionally, Nobel Prize–winning Israeli American psychologist Daniel Kahneman found that people would rather do business with a person they like and trust rather than someone they do not, even if the likeable person is offering a lower-quality product or service at a higher price.[4]

Tom Peters, author of *In Search of Excellence*, is quoted as saying that success in business today is 15 percent technology and 85 percent EI.[5] It certainly stands to reason then that 15 percent of overall job success is related to technical skills and 85 percent to EI. Those numbers are surprising, especially since traditional hiring practices reflect a focus on technical skills. The screening of applicants, the interview process, interview questions, and reference checking are geared toward technical skills. At best, we focus on the EI of job candidates for 15 percent of the process, and at least 85 percent is devoted to getting the person with the best technical skills and experience related to a particular job. Those percentages should be reversed based on what we know about job success from that study.

You certainly need both the technical and people skills, but more attention should be given to finding the person with the right EI. A base of technical knowledge and experience is important, but if they have the aptitude and capacity to learn, you can train and teach them the technical skills. This is not the case with the softer skills, which include your ability to work with people, character, personality, and overall likeability. It is difficult to teach someone the aspects of EI if they just do not seem to get it.

People can improve in those areas, but it is difficult to change someone's core character and value system. You can soften the edges, but you most likely are not going to make major changes. They are wired a certain way, and it will always be a struggle for them to act differently than the character traits they are equipped with. Perhaps you have heard the phrase "a leopard never changes its spots," which means it is impossible for one to change their character, even if they try very hard. The expression is sometimes stated as "a leopard cannot change its spots," which implies that no one can change their own innate nature.

People can get better at EI, it just takes time, and there will most likely be a bit of a struggle. Why not start with someone who has great EI and then train them with the technical skills you are looking for? As stated earlier, you still need to make sure there is a base of technical knowledge and ability, as well as the capability and aptitude for the work.

PARENTAL DISCIPLINE

Perhaps one way to illustrate the concept of "from the heart" is to look at the way parents discipline their children. It should be noted that the principles for good conversation from this book are ones that will work in parenting. If you already have children or are planning to, you already know, or will know, that you are going to have many challenging conversations with your children.

Growing up there were multiple occasions where Carly was disciplined and punished. During those times, her parents would often use the phrase, "This hurts me more than it hurts you." At that particular time, she would have vehemently disagreed, but she did not want to extend the punishment so she kept her mouth shut.

When she had children of her own, she knew full well what her parents were talking about when they made that statement. It is painful to see people that you care about and love in pain or discomfort. The point is, however, that the punishment is given out of care and love. The parent knows that the child is being protected from greater pain or hurt. The parent knows that if the child listens to and heeds the warnings and advice, it is much better for them in the long run.

Discipline is often necessary in parenting and the workplace. Discipline done out of concern for the individual, with a sense of humility, can be very effective. The end goal is to help people become better versions of themselves. Keeping the end goal in mind is paramount and more important than your own feelings and uncomfortableness.

KIND BUT TRUTHFUL

Caring for the person you are conversing with does not mean you cannot be honest. In fact, when you are frank and truthful, you show the person that you truly value them. You show great worth in the person if you are able to provide honest feedback. The truth must be delivered in the right way. As they say, "The truth hurts." Yes, it might be hurtful, but sharing the truth in a heartfelt and caring way is possible. People typically appreciate honesty if it is delivered with honorable intent and especially if a trusting relationship already exists.

When delivering truth that might be difficult or painful to hear, you may want to start the conversation with a comment something like this: "I am guessing that what I have to say may be difficult to hear, but I want to share it with you because I care about you and I believe it will be helpful to you. You may see if differently, but based on my observations (include the specific details), this is the conclusion I have reached. Do you see it the same or differently?" It is helpful to just put it out there right away. Acknowledge that you understand what they may be experiencing.

One of the leaders Luke had the opportunity to work with throughout the years was great at being honest. It was Luke's boss, and his name was Jesse. Jesse could quickly size up a situation and a person, and determine the flaws in the person's approach to a particular situation or problem. Jesse would confront the person with the truth as he saw it. His delivery could be described as a sledgehammer approach to sharing the truth. He was typically right on with his assessment, but because of his delivery method, the message was rarely received successfully. The truth that could have helped the person was not viewed as helpful by the recipient because of the way it was delivered. Although the message might have been given out of heartfelt care for the individual, because that care was not effectively conveyed, the benefit of the truth and the message was not received. It was unfortunate for both parties.

Working with Jesse for quite some time, Luke was the recipient of brutal but honest feedback more than once. Throughout time he was able to "thicken his skin" and use the feedback to better himself. The feedback was usually painful, but it was typically legitimate and right on. The point is, this individual's approach is not an example of what it means to speak from the heart. To be effective, delivering difficult truths and information must be done in a kind and respectful way.

As Luke continued to work with this individual, he came to realize that Jesse cared about him, and that is why he shared frank and honest feedback with him. He wanted to make Luke better. Because Luke was able to look past the delivery and see the message, he was able to grow and change for his own betterment.

For individuals who did not work with Jesse on a regular basis or for any extended period of time, the honest feedback was not well received. There was nothing in the delivery of the information that indicated Jesse cared. Consequently, the individuals never took the feedback to heart because of the way the message was conveyed. It appeared that Jesse was just mean, nasty, and demoralizing. Take note, the only way a message delivered in that way has any chance of being effectively received is if there is a strong, deep, and long-standing relationship between the deliverer and the receiver.

Unfortunately, many individuals could have learned and grown tremendously from Jesse's feedback. Jesse was an intelligent individual and had a knack for sizing things up. He had a critical eye that was always able to see a way that something could be improved upon. If he had conveyed his messages in a truthful but kind way, the results would have been much different. You need to strive to find a way to be frank but respectful. It may take a lot of thought and practice, but most individuals will appreciate the truth if delivered appropriately.

A greeting card company has developed a line of cards that carry a short and franker message than traditional cards. The intent of these cards is that they will start conversations. Susan's mother had just died of cancer. She received one of these cards from her friend Brian. The card was blank inside except for two words: "Cancer Sucks." This card meant more to Sue than any of the other cards she got because it got to the core of how she felt. The message was frank and honest, and delivered from someone who cared.

Most times the truth does hurt, but it can be delivered in a way that provides an opportunity for learning and growth. Do not let your important message get lost because of poor delivery.

SHARING VULNERABILITIES

A great way to have a meaningful conversation is by sharing some of your own vulnerabilities. It is not something you want to lead the conversation with, but there are often appropriate times during a conversation that you can share something that shows you are not perfect. People will appreciate when you share mistakes that you have made and how you handled them. Sharing vulnerabilities is powerful and effective.

This point is clearly illustrated in the book by Patrick Lencioni called *Getting Naked*.[6] The book is a fable that looks at two different consulting companies and each of their unique business approaches and vastly different cultures. The one company's approach is all about, "We are the experts and we always have all the answers. After all, that's why we are in business." The other firm's culture and approach is all about listening to the customer, admitting that they do not have all the answers, and being responsive. This firm shows their vulnerabilities to the customer, hence the title, *Getting Naked*.

The one firm's approach to serving clients is to show vulnerability and complete transparency. They have an attitude of caring about others, listening to their needs and wants, asking questions, and being real. They do not oversell and are willing to lose the job. The clients and the employees are happy and satisfied. The other firm's approach is to strive to prove their competency and intellectual prowess to their clients. Their employees are stressed and not as happy.

Although the two consulting firms are offering some of the same services, they have very different approaches. A management consultant ends up trying to merge the two companies, and the book recounts his discoveries along the way. His discoveries are fascinating and a bit surprising. The firm that shows vulnerability and does not oversell is much more productive, not only financially, but also in other ways.

Through this fable, as told by Lencioni, the management consultant discovers and learns a lot about the two different cultures. Lencioni boils it down to three fear concepts that held the one firm back: the fear of losing the business, the fear of being embarrassed, and the fear of feeling inferior. Lencioni shares ways to combat those fears to work toward ultimate success. He explains such concepts as

- telling the kind truth
- celebrating your mistakes
- making everything about the client
- consulting instead of selling

The advice Lencioni offers to business is applicable to conversations and relationships as well. These concepts tie in perfectly with the concepts of speaking from the heart.

SUMMARY

Speaking from the heart is an important concept for building trust. Trust is built through heartfelt conversations and is at the core of authentic relationships. Heartfelt conversations must be frank and honest but delivered in a way that reflects a desire to be of service to an individual. Speaking from the heart supposes that you take a risk and are willing to share your own vulnerabilities. Sharing, conversing, and building relationships in this way has the potential for many more rewards than risks. Let your guard down, relax your own self-importance, and enjoy being real.

CHAPTER 5 RECAP

Speaking from the heart

- is a way of communicating that reflects care for others, a sense of humility, and service above self
- is meaningful communication and heartfelt conversation that blends the language of the brain and the heart
- uses the core competencies of EI—self-awareness, self-management, empathy and social awareness, and relationship management
- is a way of delivering the truth in a kind and caring manner
- involves sharing your vulnerabilities

NOTES

1. Daniel Goleman, *Emotional Intelligence* (New York: Bantam, 1995).
2. "Emotional and Social Intelligence Leadership Qualities," Key Step Media, April 11, 2017. Accessed June 25, 2019, https://www.keystepmedia.com/emotional-social-intelligence-leadership-competencies/.
3. Keld Jensen, "Intelligence Is Overrated: What You Really Need to Succeed," *Forbes*, April 12, 2012. Accessed July 18, 2019, https://www.forbes.com/sites/keldjensen/2012/04/12/intelligence-is-overrated-what-you-really-need-to-succeed/#1a219826b6d2.
4. Rabbi David Wolpe, "Why Americans Are so Angry about Everything," *Time*, January 5, 2016. Accessed July 18, 2019, https://time.com/4166326/why-americans-are-so-angry-about-everything/.
5. "Emotional Intelligence Assessments," Lead Mark Coaching, 2017. Accessed July 18, 2019, www.leadmarkcoaching.com/emotional-intelligence-assessments/.
6. Patrick Lencioni, *Getting Naked: A Business Fable about Shedding the Three Fears That Sabotage Client Loyalty* (San Francisco, CA: Jossey-Bass, 2010).

Chapter Six

Listen for Understanding

> To say that a person feels listened to means a lot more than just their ideas get heard. It's a sign of respect. It makes people feel valued.
>
> —Deborah Tannen

Most of us have heard the saying, "God gave us two ears and only one mouth." In fact, we have heard it countless times and yet still need to be reminded of the message of that adage. The simple message is that we should put twice the amount of effort into listening than we do speaking. It is the idea that listening is much more important than speaking. The quote is originally attributed to Epictetus, a Greek Stoic philosopher who lived from 50 AD to 135 AD. He is quoted as saying, "We have two ears and one mouth so that we can listen twice as much as we speak."

Listening is much bigger than just keeping your ears open and your mouth shut. "Listening means taking a vigorous, human interest in what is being told us," said poet Alice Duer Miller. "You can listen like a blank wall or like a splendid auditorium where every sound comes back fuller and richer."[1]

According to a University of Missouri Extension report, studies show that 70 to 80 percent of our day is spent in some form of communication. The results of the study reflect that on average 9 percent was spent writing, 16 percent reading, 30 percent speaking, and 45 percent listening.[2] Various studies stress the importance of listening as a communication skill. Of the four skills (writing, reading, speaking, and listening), listening is the one we get no training in. The fact that we get no or little training on how to effectively listen is a problem.

Another issue stems from the fact that we generally speak at a rate of 125 words per minute but have the mental capacity to understand at a rate of 400 words per minute. Because we have that excess mental capacity, the result is that our minds tend to wander and we think about other things. Knowing that, we need to be extra careful to concentrate and keep our focus on the conversation.

To listen does not necessarily mean that you are silent. Active listening by nature involves asking questions for clarification and sometimes repeating what you have heard. According to Businessdictionary.com, active listening is the "act of mindfully hearing and attempting to comprehend the meaning of words spoken by another in a conversation or speech."[3]

Active listening is an important business communication skill, and it can involve making sounds that indicate attentiveness, as well as the listener giving feedback in the form of a paraphrased rendition of what has been said by the other party for their confirmation. Listening means that the individual has your undivided attention. You are focused on them and what they are saying. The goal is to totally understand them and the message they are delivering. That seems to be so difficult for us.

Many of us cannot wait to impart our wisdom so we rush to "understand" them while we are formulating a profound response, which may include our perceived wise advice. In fact, we are focused on making sure they understand us and not the reverse. It almost becomes a competition of sorts. Who will have the winning thoughts?

Practice and use the phrase, "If I hear you right you are saying (insert the details). Is that correct?" When they respond, do not allow them to give a simple response or head nod. Also, be careful of a simple "yes" response. It may just be because they do not feel comfortable. Look at their body language and their tone—do they mean it or are they just afraid to correct you? Your body language and tone can help make them more comfortable in being honest with you. Repeat what they are saying, and, when possible, use another similar situation or example to help clarify. This is important—you need to understand where they are coming from.

LISTENING TIPS

Keep in mind the following seven tips as you enter a conversation. They can be helpful in making sure you listen with intent and proper focus.

- Make eye contact.
- Be present in the conversation.
- Be nonjudgmental.
- Listen to the words.
- Do not interrupt the speaker.
- Ask clarifying questions.
- Pay attention to what is not said.

Make Eye Contact

Looking at the speaker is the first indication that you have given them your attention. Eye contact is important, just be careful that it is not awkward. Staring too long may make the person nervous. You will need to evaluate the person that is speaking to see if they are comfortable with eye contact. You should make the attempt and see how it is received. If you sense that the eye contact is making them uncomfortable, you may need to adjust your approach. At the very least, you can face them in terms of your body position.

Making eye contact during a conversation is appropriate and expected in most Western cultures; however, there are some cultures where looking the person in the eyes is viewed differently. In many Middle Eastern cultures, eye contact is less common and considered less appropriate as compared to U.S. culture. This is especially true with eye contact between sexes. But in those same cultures intense eye contact between those of the same gender is a sign that you are being truthful and genuine. It is important that you understand the nuances that exist among the people you have conversations with. You can never assume that they have the same views and understanding as you do.

Be Present in the Conversation

Body language is one way of making sure you are sending the message to the person that is speaking that you are engaged in the conversation. Part of being present is being aware of the distance between you—the listener—and the speaker. Be mindful of what the appropriate distance is. To demonstrate good listening skills you have to be sensitive to the other person. The appropriate distance between the speaker and the listener varies from one person to another. The comfortable amount of space between the speaker and the listener depends on the comfort level of the other person. It also depends on how well you know the person, the amount of trust that exists between you and the other person, the type of relationship that exists, and the culture. The average comfort level is one and a half to three feet for family and friends, three to ten feet for casual acquaintances and coworkers, and more than four feet for total strangers.

There are people who invade the personal space of people they are talking to. It creates a very uncomfortable situation. It adds an additional level of difficulty to the conversation. If you are the one who's space is being compromised, you end up being more focused on the uncomfortable feeling than actually listening. Your efforts are spent figuring out how you can back away or leave the conversation altogether.

Be Nonjudgmental

A good listener listens without passing judgment on what is being said. Verbalizing the judgment is not productive in a good conversation. Thinking judgmental thoughts is not conducive to a genuine listening experience either. If you are passing judgment you are not listening to what someone is saying. You have already made up your mind, and it will affect your ability to listen objectively. There will be a time when you can tactfully share your thoughts, but while you are actively listening is not the time.

Listen to the Words

This seems obvious; however, so many times we are not hearing what the speaker is saying. We may be listening but not actually hearing the words they are saying. Sometimes it is helpful to picture what they are saying. The idea is that you are intent on the words they are speaking. It is helpful to visualize their story. You have most likely encountered an individual who speaks the same language but has a strong accent that is different than yours or has a speech impediment as the result of a stroke, or someone who is very soft-spoken. Think about how intently you have to listen to that person. Sometimes it can be exhausting because you are so focused on listening with an attempt to figure out what they are saying. All listening should be done with that intensity.

Do Not Interrupt the Speaker

Interrupting the speaker is not only rude to the one doing the speaking, but also it interrupts and distracts you, the listener. If you are figuring out what you want to say, that means you are not paying close attention to the speaker. Let the speaker finish before offering your comments. It is okay if there is a period of silence between the time the speaker stops and when the listener responds. If you are so anxious to offer your solution or idea you will not be attentive to the speaker. Wait for the speaker to pause before you begin speaking. That way you can give your undivided attention to the speaker. There are times that it is appropriate to find a way to tactfully interrupt a speaker. This is especially true for those individuals who can talk nonstop and never take a break. If that is you, be conscious of it and guard against doing it. It makes it difficult for the listener to actively listen when the speaker drones on and on. There is a limit to our attention span.

In fact, a recent study by Microsoft found that the average human being has an attention span of eight seconds, down from twelve seconds in 2000. The average attention span is decreasing by 88 percent each year. At eight seconds, human beings now have a shorter attention span than a goldfish, which is nine seconds.[4] This is alarming, but it is a sign of the digitalized times. It is a fact that must be considered from the point of view of both the speaker and the listener. If you are the speaker you must be aware of this, and certainly as the listener you will have to work extra hard to pay attention to the conversation.

If you need to interrupt, you should be able to find a way to cut them off after a reasonable amount of time. This book is about conversation, and it takes two to have a conversation. A one-way "conversation" is nothing more than a speech.

Ask Clarifying Questions

Asking clarifying questions is helpful, but you need to wait until the pause so that you do not derail the conversation. Asking a question may take the conversation into an entirely different place if the question conjures up something different in the person doing the speaking. If someone's name (who you know) comes up in a conversation, you may be tempted to interrupt the conversation. You may say, "By the way, how is so and so," and then the conversation will most likely go in a totally different direction. The speaker is now thinking about that person and not their original message.

When the speaker pauses, ask clarifying questions. Although it is not necessarily a question, it is good to start with a clarifying statement. For instance, if someone comes to you to complain about another individual at work and is asking for your assistance, you should listen and then repeat back in summary form what you thought you heard them say. Something like, "So if I heard you correctly, you said that you were really upset when Mary didn't pick up your phone when it was ringing and you were on break. You believe that you had an agreement with her that when you were not at your desk, she would pick up your phone. Because she did not pick up your phone you missed a very important call. That is what I heard you say, is that correct or did you say something different?" You can then follow up with some clarifying questions. "How long ago did you make the agreement with Mary to pick up your phone in your absence?" "Did you approach Mary about why she did not pick up your phone?" "What follow-up do you think would be helpful?" This shows that you were listening and that you care about the situation and take it seriously. Obviously, it is serious to the one who is bringing it to your attention.

If there are chances to do so throughout the conversation, it is good to give regular feedback. Watch for natural places to offer feedback. Giving feedback during the conversation lets the speaker know you are truly listening. Feedback might be verbal or nonverbal. Shaking your head in acknowledgment is one way of giving that feedback. You can also use facial expressions to show that you get what they are saying, that you identify with the emotions associated with the story they are telling.

In terms of verbal feedback, you can interject short, simple words or phrases like the following:

- "Wow, that is awesome."
- "Oh, I'm sorry to hear that."
- "Yes, I know."
- "I heard the same thing."
- "Good point."

Use short, generic words and phrases, as you do not want to change the other person's thought pattern by introducing an off-topic question or a different idea. There will be time for that later on. For now, what you want to do is hear them out.

Pay Attention to What Is Not Said

Do not miss the message that is not stated. Sometimes the message is more about what is not said than what is said. Observe the body language. For example, does the body language convey a sense of relaxation or stress? Look at their facial expression. What story does it tell? Does it conjure up a look of happiness, sadness, anger, or some other emotion? Listen to the tone of their voice. Does it sound excited, depressed, happy, ambivalent, or angry?

The idea of what is not being said will also depend on how wordy the person is who is doing the speaking. Some people use very few words, while others are much more verbose. For those who are less wordy, you may have to fill in more of the blanks or pay attention to the nonverbal cues. In every case, it is good to make sure you clarify the message you think they were trying to deliver. The message is determined by the words that were spoken, as well as the nonverbal cues you observed.

Practice active listening in social situations so that it becomes more natural and easier to accomplish in a professional or work setting. It is not always easy to resist the natural tendency to talk about yourself, but authentic relationships are built on your interest in others. Ask the other person about themselves. It is rare for people to respond with one- or two-word answers and not be engaged. People tend to like talking about themselves and appreciate your interest in them.

Keep in mind that authentic relationships are built on ongoing conversations. The "listening" aspect of the conversation is more than half of that interaction. Being a good listener is an integral part of the components of authentic relationships. The foundational factors of authentic relationships are as follows:

- A foundation of trust
- Acceptance of who someone is and their life status at any point in time
- Acknowledging that the other person may think differently
- A willingness to give and take—being willing to give more than you may get
- Expressed expectations
- A commitment—being willing to overcome obstacles

SUMMARY

At the core of this active listening concept, like the other principles outlined in this book, is a fundamental and genuine respect and concern for people. It is the value and importance you place in others as you help them lead productive and successful lives. You can only do that by actively listening to who they are, what they need, where they have been, and where they are at this point in time. Every life matters, every life has value, and time invested in others is a noble, worthy, and rewarding cause. Without this at your core, implementing these listening mind-sets for conducting and facilitating difficult but beneficial conversations will be just an unproductive exercise since you will just be going through the motions.

CHAPTER 6 RECAP

- It is important to conscientiously remind yourself as you continue through a conversation to resist the urge to formulate the next thing you want to say while the other person is talking.
- Remember that you often come to the conversation with preconceived notions of the other person's perspective and mind-set; suspend those preconceived notions for purposes of the conversation.
- Do not allow yourself to formulate your opinion and course of action prior to the conversation.
- Listening for understanding means that you let the other person talk. It is as simple as that. When you do not totally get it or understand, you need to ask questions and then listen again. Keep asking questions until you get it. Do not move on until you have clarity.
- Remember to repeat back what you think you have heard.

NOTES

1. Alice Duer Miller, quoted in Richard Nordquist, "The Definition of Listening and How to Do It Well," ThoughtCo., January 6, 2019. Accessed July 19, 2019, https://www.thoughtco.com/listening-communication-term-1691247.

2. Dick Lee and Delmar Hatesohl, "Listening: Our Most Used Communication Skill," MU Extension, n.d. Accessed June 25, 2019, https://extension2.missouri.edu/cm150.

3. "Active Listening," Business Dictionary, n.d. Accessed June 25, 2019, http://www.businessdictionary.com/definition/active-listening.html.

4. Kevin McSpadden, "You Now Have a Shorter Attention Span Than a Goldfish," *Time*, May 14, 2015. Accessed June 25, 2019, https://time.com/3858309/attention-spans-goldfish/.

Chapter Seven

Allow for Differences

> Not everyone thinks the way you think, knows the things you know, believes the things you believe, nor acts the way you would act. Remember this and you will go a long way in getting along with people.
> —Arthur Forman

We tend to like people who are like us, and it is much easier to deal with them. We typically spend time with people who share our interests, beliefs, and values. It is more difficult to relate to individuals who are different than us; therefore, we do not spend time with them.

The fact that they are different adds an extra layer of difficulty to interactions with them. Conversations are not as easy. The level of the challenge in the conversation is typically driven by how similar or how different the individuals are. The personality of the individual enters the equation as well. Even with drastic differences in beliefs, interests, and values, some people have a personality that makes those differences easier to take.

Then there are others who have a personality that may just clash with yours. They get on your nerves. Conversations with those individuals pose an even bigger challenge. Conversations are a struggle with people who are different than us. And we are all different.

WHY THE STRUGGLE?

At some level we all struggle with accepting, acknowledging, and dealing with differences in others. Granted some people are better than others at dealing with it. It is just another "difference" based on personality, background, and experiences. We all need to be reminded from time to time to hold our judgment, suspend certainty, and truly enter the conversation with an open mind.

Why is it a struggle? Even though we try to acknowledge it in our minds, our actions and behaviors do not typically follow suit. Perhaps it is because, for most of us, it is easier to process and deal with things if we see them as right or wrong, black or white. We tend to hang around people who see things the way we do. Why is that?

Our perceptions and perspectives, the differences, have been formed throughout the years through our experiences and interactions. The older you are, the more experiences and interactions you have had. Those experiences and interactions oftentimes continue to validate your perceptions and perspectives. Our family, friends, and colleagues often validate them.

Face it, we are typically attracted to people who share our beliefs and values. We typically do not seek out people who stretch our thinking, individuals who cause us to question our core beliefs, perspectives, perceptions, and values. We are steeped in the way we see things and tend to discount the affect that has on our interactions with others.

WHAT MAKES US DIFFERENT

Before we tackle strategies for allowing for differences in the conversation, let us consider those things that make us different. There are five major "uniqueness" factors that make us different:

1. gender
2. ethnicity and culture
3. family background
4. personality
5. experiences

Gender

Society has changed a great deal, but most people are still influenced by the traditional view of gender. Many people grow up with preconceived notions about the role, conduct, and position of each gender class.

Psychologists have proven that the right and left hemispheres of the male and female brains are not set up in exactly the same way. In general, there are differences in the way men and women listen and express feelings, to name just a few. These differences are not better or worse, just different. There are obviously biological differences as well. Generally speaking, there are physical, emotional, and thought processing differences between the genders. Couple that with the way people perceive the differences in their own heads and you have one big factor in the "what makes us different" equation.

Relative to gender, societal norms have changed dramatically during the past several years. The lines between genders are not as clear. In some respects, this minimizes the differences, and in other ways it makes the gap wider. Your perspective determines whether it minimizes the differences or creates a bigger divide because you see it differently. You need to acknowledge that others may view the gender factor in a totally different way than you do.

Ethnicity and Culture

Each country has their own unique characteristics. Even within the United States there are a myriad of cultures. Each ethnicity and culture brings with it things that set it apart from other groups. The identification with one group or another creates differences among us. People are marked by their ethnicity and culture.

Again, as societal norms change, we can see how these differences can be reduced. As we blend ethnic and cultural differences through cross-cultural marriages and having children, these lines become less and less clear. Again, for many it minimizes the difference, while for others who see it differently, it creates a bigger divide. It is not necessarily right or wrong, it is just different.

Family Background

The first definition listed for family on Dictionary.com is a "basic social unit consisting of parents and their children, considered as a group, whether dwelling together or not."[1] For many years, the traditional family was considered to be a father, a mother, and their offspring, the children. Parents had certain standards and beliefs, and they imposed them upon their children. For the most part, each child was treated the same. Today, there are more nontraditional family units than there are traditional.

Generally speaking, family members have had the same experiences and upbringing; therefore, it is natural that they share the same beliefs and worldviews. In cases where a family member does not share the same belief system, it often causes family strife. Family life or lack thereof has a profound impact on someone's beliefs and values. What they were taught, what they saw (compared to what they were told), and family interactions play a part in determining who we are.

Family traditions affect how we see things. What was normal to us growing up might not have been normal for the person we are conversing with. Birth order, the number of siblings, the gender of those siblings, the age gap between siblings, and the number of parents and their gender (one or two or two of each) play a part in who we are. Think of all the differences between family situations, and you will realize why these differences tend to create a multitude of obstacles to communication and a good conversation.

Personality

According to Myers-Briggs, there are sixteen major personality types. The sixteen personality types were created by Isabel Myers and Katharine Briggs as a way to categorize an individual according to their preferred way of thinking and behaving. These determinations were made by Myers-Briggs in the 1960s based on the work of psychologist Carl Jung. The sixteen personality types are a further delineation of the four key dimensions that can be used to categorize people. The four key dimensions are as follows:

- introversion versus extraversion
- sensing versus intuition
- thinking versus feeling
- judging versus perceiving[2]

Even if we agreed that everyone we meet falls neatly into one of the sixteen personality types, interactions among the people from the different types would be difficult. With more than 7.5 billion people in this world, it is unlikely that you would find two people who have identical personalities. You might get really close, but there would still be some differences.

If you are a parent and you have two or more children, you have seen for yourself the differences in personality. Two children from the same parents, growing up in the same household, separated in age by a year or two typically have two very different personalities. As an example, three children from the same parents, two years apart in age, two boys and one girl, growing up in the same exact house, with the same set of rules and upbringing end up with three distinct personalities. One personality may be distinctly like the personality of one parent or the other, and one or more of them could be an equal blend of both parents.

The point is, our personality is unique and at the core of who we are. It has a tremendous influence on how we act and react in conversation with others. Remember that the individual you are talking to is likely to have a totally different personality than you. The two of you may not even fall into one of the same four key dimensions mentioned earlier. Remember too that sometimes the very things that annoy us in others are the characteristics we ourselves exhibit.

As parents you may have experienced the notion that the child who seems to exhibit personality traits similar to your own sometimes seems more difficult to deal with. What we see in them is our own flaws, and we want to change them. Embracing a child's unique characteristics is much better than trying to force them into a mold that suits us. We are all born with certain personality traits. As new parents you may have discovered that the baby seems to come prewired or preprogrammed with a certain personality and that you have little to no control of much of that. Just like personalities within a family sometimes create turmoil and unique challenges, so it is with our interactions within the workplace and other social settings.

Different personalities coming together to have a meaningful conversation can be a beautiful experience. Embrace the uniqueness of one another. Remember, as you have that interaction and that conversation, someone's innate personality is not right or wrong, it is just different.

Experiences

Each person has a different set of experiences. Everyone has a different mix or combination of good experiences and bad experiences. In fact, the same experience might be viewed very differently by two people. Something that is a good experience for one person might be a bad experience for someone else. Even for the same person, the same experience might be seen as good or bad depending on the timing of the happening relative to their life circumstances at that point in time. It is an understatement to say that we all have had unique and different life experiences. These experiences have shaped our lives and continue to reshape them as we continue along life's journey.

As you enter a conversation, remember that the message you are delivering is being received by someone who likely has had very different experiences than you. As you choose your words, remember that what they hear will be interpreted through their "experience lens." Remember that you and they have had different experiences, and keep in mind that oftentimes we may have had little to no control of those circumstances.

As you communicate with others, be conscious that their experiences are a factor as they listen to what you say and respond. The words they use and the way they explain things are related to their experiences. The experiences could be fresh and recent, or they could have happened a long time ago but still feel fresh and are ever-present in their mind. Take these things into consideration as you allow for differences.

Given the varying factors of gender, culture, family, personality, and experience, is it any wonder that we enter any general conversation with lots of impediments to a clear transfer of ideas, information, advice, thoughts, and feelings? Add to that mix a conversation that is forced because of a difficult and challenging circumstance, and you have a formula for disaster.

That is why it is so important to learn how to prevent the differences from standing in the way of a good conversation. You need to focus on the goal. The goal is to have a meaningful conversation that results in a positive outcome. The desired outcome might be a behavior change, a repaired relationship, clarification of expectations, or an overall understanding for moving forward.

WHAT IS DIFFERENT?

The things that make us different result in variations in the way we see things. The way we view the world is based on our values and beliefs, perceptions, and opinions. These values, perceptions, and opinions are developed and continue to develop from our uniqueness factors described earlier.

Values

The *Oxford Dictionary* defines values as a "person's principles or standards of behavior, one's judgment of what is important in life." Other words that could be used to describe someone's values are ethics, morals, or rules of conduct. Values differ from person to person. Each person's values are determined and shaped by familial, cultural, and experiential influences. Not everyone shares the same values and beliefs because of those influences.

Keep in mind also that people's values are typically not static. Most people's values change throughout time based on new and different experiences. Acknowledge and accept the fact that what you believe to be the appropriate standard of behavior may not be the same as it is for someone else. What they believe to be the most important things in life may be very different than what you deem to be the most important.

Perceptions

The *Oxford Dictionary* defines perception as the "ability to see, hear, or become aware of something through the senses. It is the way in which something is regarded, understood, or interpreted." Two key words stand out. The two key words are *senses* and *interpretation*.

Our senses are unique and different. Some people may have a keen sense of hearing, while others may have keen eyesight. These are determined through family genetics, as well as family and life experiences, and are sometimes affected by medical and physical conditions.

The way we interpret things varies from person to person as well. People perceive things differently. Our perceptions are influenced by our individual differences and preconceived notions. We choose to select different aspects of a message to focus our attention on based on what interests us, what is familiar to us, and what we consider to be important.

How many unique things can different people see when they look at the exact same thing? Take a blank piece of white paper with a red dot in the center of it. Ask one hundred people what they see and you are likely to get twenty different answers. You may say, "Well, that is silly. There's only one right answer. It is a red dot." That is your perception. You are interpreting it from your sense of sight, and your answer is, "It is a red dot." Someone else might answer that it is the center of a bull's eye, and another person might see a drop of blood.

Your answer is based on how you interpret what you see. It is an image that seems so simple, yet it is perceived differently by different people. Perceptions are different for each of us. The sooner we can come to grips with that concept and accept it, the better off we will be as we interact with others.

Accepting someone else's perception is especially difficult for some people. We consider ourselves rational and intelligent people, and so we assume that the way we interpret something is the right way and any other way is wrong. In terms of the red dot example, just because you think the only possible answer is that it is a "red dot" does not make it so.

A conversation may involve a few of the senses. Sight is certainly one of them. In addition, conversations are somewhat based on the sense of hearing. People interpret what they hear, and that may be completely different than what you think you are saying and different than what you think they are hearing.

Opinions

An opinion is defined by the *Oxford Dictionary* as a "view or judgment formed about something not necessarily based on fact or knowledge. An estimation of the quality or worth of someone or something." Perhaps you have heard the catchphrase, "Opinions are like belly buttons, everybody has them." Yes, we all have opinions and are often willing to share them as if they are facts. Varying opinions can create a great deal of turmoil and disagreement.

A simple example is fashion. Not everyone agrees on what "looks good." Your opinion of what looks good is based on your culture, your upbringing, the media, your friends, and a myriad of other influences. You may look at someone's attire and say, "Well that shirt just does not go with those pants. It just does not look good. Why would they even wear that?" Most likely the person wearing that outfit does not see it the same way. You may consider it a fact, but it is just your opinion. You may believe something makes someone look heavy or short or washed out, while someone else may see it totally differently. Because you see it a certain way, you treat it as if it is fact. We take great pride in our opinions and often consider them to be facts. Conversely, we view other people's opinions as misguided and wrong.

In Christian circles, there have long been arguments about which version of the Bible is correct. There is a large contingent that believes the King

James version of the Bible is the only authentic and correct version and therefore the only one that should be used. This issue has split churches.

The fact is that the King James version is one translation among many. The fact is that the original Bible was written in Hebrew, Aramaic, and Greek, and unless you go back to the original texts you are using a translation. Your opinion may be that the King James version is the most accurate, but that is your opinion. All versions of the Bible (and there are literally hundreds of them) are the result of an individual or group of individuals who translated the original Hebrew, Aramaic, and Greek words into a more current language and understandable document.

Some have tried to make the argument that one version or translation is inspired by God Himself, but again, that would be an opinion, as there is no factual evidence of that. Quite frankly, each translation is someone's (or some group's) interpretation of the text from the original languages based on their study of those languages, the culmination of their own life experiences, and their understanding of the culture present when the books of the Bible were originally written.

Our opinions are not the facts, they are just our opinions, and we need to keep that in perspective. It is not effective in conversations to force our opinions on others or convey that they are facts. Moreover, it is not helpful to discount others' opinions and treat them as if they are misguided.

WE ARE ALL DIFFERENT

We have looked at the differences among us and what causes those differences to exist. There is really no getting around those variations. When you look at the potential diversities it can feel overwhelming. How can we possibly carry on a conversation or build a relationship with someone who may have so many different values, perceptions, and opinions than our own?

The distinctions exist and need to be acknowledged, dealt with, and perhaps even embraced. The world is a much more interesting place because of our differences. It is hard to imagine a world full of people who are alike. Movies have been made about that concept. One such movie is *The Stepford Wives*, based on the book with the same title by Ira Levin. *The Stepford Wives* is about a small suburb where the women happily go about their housework—cleaning, cooking, and doing laundry—all to please their husbands. A new family to the quaint little town of Stepford, Connecticut, soon discovers the sinister truth. The truth is that the wives have been replaced by robots who act alike and in strict obedience to their husbands. It is a scary concept and one that thankfully does not reflect reality.

WHAT CAN BE DONE?

There are things you can do to make it easier to accept differences in other people. If you allow yourself to experience new things and new people, it will make it easier and more natural. Chances are the new thinking will prevent the differences from getting in the way of a meaningful conversation. There are three things that you can do: 1) Get to know the other person; 2) understand and accept others' beliefs, values, opinions, and perceptions; and 3) expand your circle of friends and interactions. These practices will expand your thinking and make it easier to carry on meaningful conversations.

Get to Know the Person

There was a tragic situation in Pittsburgh on October 27, 2018, at a synagogue where eleven people were killed. There is a great anonymous quote that was published, in response to that heartbreaking situation: "Let's start having conversations . . . it's hard to hate someone you know." The quote certainly makes a good point. What can be done to make sure you "allow for differences"? The best thing to do is to get to know the person. Get to know their background, their experiences, their values, and what makes them tick. You do that through conversation.

Just because you accept the differences does not mean that you agree with them. There are differences between acceptance, agreement, and approval. You need to accept the person even though you may not agree with their philosophy or approve of their actions. The key is to accept the person and the differences. This will be easier as you get to know the person.

As you get to know the person, it is likely that you will find at least one thing that you have in common. It may be an experience you have both encountered. It may be someone you both know. It may be similar family background. Look for that one thing that creates a connection. Obviously, some people are easier to connect with than others, but eventually most people become "connectable."

Once you get to know the person you will be more apt to be able to tolerate and perhaps even embrace their differences. There are countless stories of people who have passed judgment on a person based on a first impression only to find that the first impression was totally wrong. Deep friendships have developed between individuals that at first glance seemed to make the unlikeliest of compatible companions. Take a risk, get to know the person, and you may be surprised what you might find out.

Accept Others' Belief Systems, Perspectives, and Opinions

Uniqueness is a gift. Each of us is different and unique in our own special way. We all have strengths and weaknesses. We spend a lot of time focusing on and trying to correct others' weaknesses, as well as our own (if we admit we have them). A great book that deals with the uniqueness of each individual and the perceived weaknesses is *Freak Factor*, written by David Rendall. The author stresses that many times our weaknesses are what make us unique, and we need to capitalize on them and figure out how they can be used as a strength.[3] We need to stop trying to conform everyone to what we believe they should be.

There may be times when you feel like you are compromising your own belief system if you acknowledge and accept that someone has a differing belief. You may think, "If I acknowledge and try to understand their position, I am condoning and encouraging them to think in a way that I believe is wrong."

Do you have the right to decide that they are wrong? Even if you answered yes to that question, you need to think about how that stance helps you in moving toward a solution. Most likely it will create an obstacle that becomes almost insurmountable. Acknowledging and accepting the difference does not compromise your position or condone theirs.

It is perfectly fine to admit that there are certain things that are right or wrong. For instance, the laws of the land. It does not matter how you were brought up or what your opinion is, it is illegal to violate the law. If you do break the law, there will be consequences.

Trying to understand someone else's position, inquiring about their perceptions, or showing interest in their opinion does not signal your agreement with their position. You can certainly be up-front about your thoughts and beliefs. You may start the conversation by saying, "Could you tell me more about why you believe that? I have a totally different view than that, but I would be interested to know and understand your thinking." Notice that the question is posed to them first. It shows that you are interested in them and that you value them as an individual.

Those statements in reverse order send a totally different message. Those statements reversed send a message that you cannot wait to tell them why they are wrong in their thinking, but you will pretend you care about them by throwing in that question about why they think the way they do. Starting with the statement, "I have a totally different belief than you do," will most likely illicit a defensiveness on their part, and they may not even hear your follow-up question of inquiry.

It sounds simple and it is subtle, but it is also very powerful. Despite that it is so simple, we let our own need to be right and prove our point get in the way.

We risk damaging a relationship or losing out on developing a new one. Our need to feel validated jeopardizes a positive outcome from a conversation.

Realize that just like your viewpoint is based on your background, experiences, interaction, and many other factors, so is their viewpoint. Resist the temptation to judge them based on your mental model. Seek first to understand and then to be understood.

Expand Your Circle of "Interactions"

Another way to get more comfortable with others' differences is to expand your circle of influence. We tend to hang out with people who share our values, beliefs, and opinions. We share experiences together, which then reinforces that bond. It feels comfortable. Leave your comfort zone. To grow and improve ourselves, we often need to put ourselves in uncomfortable situations.

Expand your social circles. Resist the desire to always spend time with people who tend to be like you. Spend time with individuals who are from different backgrounds than you. Seek out activities and events that highlight and feature other cultures. There are plenty of such events—parades, ethnic food festivals, and other activities. By exposing yourself to people from other backgrounds and cultures, you will develop an understanding of and appreciation for those differences.

SUMMARY

As you enter a conversation, enter it with the understanding that there are many differences between the individuals who will be engaged in the conversation. It will help if you understand the following:

- We are all different from birth.
- We have all been shaped by our background and experiences.
- Our way is one way but not the only way.
- Our approach may not be the best approach.

Realize that the differences strengthen the conversation. Guard yourself from drawing quick conclusions about the other person and then passing judgment. Be aware of the tendency you may have to be intolerant of the differences. When you violate allowing for the differences, call yourself on it. Self-reflect and consider how you might have handled it differently. How could you handle it better the next time you are in a similar situation? These concepts are harder to grasp for some than others. The concepts of acceptance, respect, and understanding are critical to crucial, meaningful, and successful conversations. You cannot control how the other person handles the allowance for differences principles, but you can control your behavior and model appropriate actions.

CHAPTER 7 RECAP

- Remember we are all different based on gender, ethnicity and culture, family background, personality, and experience.
- Our differences cause us to have differing values, perceptions, and opinions.
- Acknowledging and accepting that those differences exist is crucial to conducting meaningful conversations. It is difficult to develop relationships if differences are seen as right or wrong.
- Realize that acknowledging and accepting differences does not mean you agree with them. It does not mean that you are condoning someone else's behavior based on those distinctions. It simply means that you understand that differences exist and you are respectful of the person despite those variances.
- What can be done? Get to know the person; it is hard to hate someone you know. Embrace the idea that uniqueness is a gift and that we are better off with differing views and opinions. Expand your circle of interactions by hanging out socially with people who are unlike you. Participate in cultural and ethnic events that are outside of your comfort zone.

NOTES

1. "Family," Dictionary.com, n.d. Accessed June 25, 2019, https://www.dictionary.com/browse/family.
2. "Myers Briggs Personality Types," Team Technology, 2019. Accessed July 19, 2019, https://www.teamtechnology.co.uk/tt/t-articl/mb-simpl.htm.
3. David Rendall, *The Freak Factor: Discovering Uniqueness by Flaunting Weakness* (Charleston, SC: Advantage Media Group, 2015).

Chapter Eight

Slow Down

> I wanted to call a time out, to demand that everybody just *stop* until I could understand everything.
> —Elizabeth Gilbert, from *Eat, Pray, Love*

Meaningful conversations take time. Crucial, results-driven conversations require meaningful exchanges. Those exchanges require us to slow down and take the time required to improve the chance of a relationship building interaction. Slow down before holding the conversation, slow down during the conversation, and slow down as you leave the conversation and reflect on the outcome.

Whether it is true or not, or even whether it would be measurable, it seems that people rarely slow down. We desire recreation and look forward to time off. We enjoy having fun and relaxing, but do we truly slow down and take a breath? Perhaps it is too painful to just slow down and sit and think. Our thoughts turn toward ourselves, and perhaps it is too upsetting to contemplate and reflect on who we really are. If we keep busy, our minds are occupied with other things, and we have no time to think, reflect, and develop a thoughtful course of action.

Whether you were religious or not, many years ago Sunday was traditionally the day when most people slowed down and enjoyed the company of others. People would sit on the porch and talk with family, friends, and neighbors. They were the conversations that "solved the problems of the world." It was very helpful to slow down and sort things out. Sometimes as we naturally talk through things, great ideas and solutions are discovered and developed.

SLOW DOWN BEFORE THE CONVERSATION

Slowing down is crucial during the conversation, but perhaps it is even more important prior to entering a conversation. It is important to think before you act. American physicist and inventor William Shockley is quoted as saying, "Regret is unnecessary. Think before you act."

Prior to the conversation, sit down and think about what you want the outcome of the conversation to be. In the case of crucial and challenging conversations this is most important. Unless you slow down and think about the context of the conversation, the purpose of the conversation, and the intended outcome of the conversation, you will just be "flying by the seat of your pants," as they say. Without thoughtful consideration and a bit of planning you may get caught up in the emotion of the moment and say or do things you may regret.

As you plan for the conversation make sure you take into account the other person. Try to consider who they are. What is their background? How are they different from you? If you do not know them all that well, do some limited and noninvasive investigation. Try to figure out what their perspective might be. Try to determine what experiences they may have had that might impact their reaction to the proposed interaction and conversation. As you contemplate the differences, prepare yourself to have an accepting attitude toward that person's differences.

Carefully consider what you want the outcome to be. What do you want as a result of the conversation? Once you have determined that, you should then think about it from the other person's perspective. Obviously, you cannot read their mind; therefore, you will not know exactly what they might expect as an outcome. But attempting to think about if from their perspective may give a different spin to your thinking. You will be guessing what their mind-set might be and what they hope will happen. It is better to guess what their perspective is than to not guess at all. Depending on the situation and the individual, you may want to ask them early on in the conversation what their expectations are.

An effective conversation planning tool is inviting a colleague or friend to critique your approach and plan. Depending on the complexity of the conversation, it may be helpful to role-play the conversation with a coworker or friend. This technique will provide another viewpoint. It will provide valuable feedback and help as you formulate the plan and make revisions and improvements that may surface as a result of the feedback.

The conversation should not be all about what you want. The measure of a truly successful conversation is when both parties leave with a certain amount of satisfaction—satisfaction that they have been heard and that there has been a reasonable and rational approach to the situation at hand. Either party may not be totally happy with the result of the conversation, but both can leave feeling understood and listened to.

If it is a disciplinary conversation, the result or outcome may be that the individual is docked a day's pay, placed on an unpaid leave, or some other form of reprimand. Even though the ramifications of their actions are reasonable and clearly outlined in some sort of code of conduct document or employee handbook, they will most likely be unhappy about the consequences of their action. If the conversation is handled properly, there is still a good chance they will understand and respect you. There is certainly no guarantee this will happen, but you need to do everything in your power to respect them enough to make sure they have had a voice in the conversation.

SLOW DOWN DURING THE CONVERSATION

During the conversation it is good to keep in mind that it is important to slow down. You need to slow down your judgment, slow down your emotions, and slow down your response. Assuming you were able to think about and plan your conversation, you should slow down so you can see if the conversation is going according to plan. It may be that your plan was not a good one. It may be that the plan will be ineffective based on the unanticipated reaction of the other party.

Do not stick to the plan if it is no longer valid. Slowing down will help you make that evaluation. If you just charge ahead with your plan regardless of what is happening in the moment, your conversation may be in vain.

Slow down and make sure you are adhering to the principles of authentic conversation outlined in this book. Make sure you are actively listening. Make sure you are suspending your judgment. Make sure you are controlling your emotions. Make sure you are doing everything you can to ensure the other party feels safe and secure.

An effective practice that helps to slow down the conversation is to take a deep breath and pause to ask questions during the interaction. Do not be afraid of silence. A few seconds of silence seems like an eternity, but it can be so powerful. It gives you time to think, reflect, assess your emotional state, and check the other person's attitude and demeanor. Pausing allows the other person to think about what you said. Suspending the conversation even for a few seconds is helpful and important, especially if it is a long, extended conversation.

Conversations can get heated as the discussion continues and difficult or sensitive information is shared. The other person may ramble on and on, and not take a breath. You are not able to control the other person's behavior. You can only control your own conduct. Hesitating or stopping your own talking may diffuse the situation. Let the other person continue on and stop and take a deep breath before you respond.

SLOW DOWN YOUR RESPONSE

In a face-to-face conversation, take the time you need before you respond. You will feel pressure to immediately respond to what the other person is saying. This pressure will be even greater if you are in a position of authority over this individual. You may think that you need to exert that authority and show how smart you are.

A much better approach is to stop and hesitate before you respond. Think about your body language and facial expressions, as well as the message you are sending. Make adjustments as necessary. Think about the words you are about to say. Are they appropriate? Will those words help or hurt the situation? Despite the awkwardness you may feel, the outcome will be enhanced by your thoughtful and careful consideration. Do not worry about the next thing on your to-do list that you have to take care of. The individual, situation, and conversation at hand deserve your time and attention.

WORLD OF TECHNOLOGY

Slowing down is a key concept when it comes to texting, e-mailing, tweeting, and other forms of posting on social media. We are bombarded by examples that demonstrate the fact that people have not slowed down before sending or posting. There are cases where the individual may have carefully considered the negative implications and sent or posted anyway. Everyone should want to be extremely careful, so we will review some guidelines that will be helpful in keeping you out of trouble.

A quick response is expected in the fast-paced world of increasing technology. We send a text and expect an immediate response. It is easy for us to send a quick response without carefully considering the message and our response. A quick text response can be problematic because you, the receiver, are assuming a certain context and "tone" to the message. You may have totally misread the intent. If you did, it is quite possible that your response will be off the mark.

Let us consider the possibility that you did misinterpret the text because you interpreted the words to mean something different than they were intended to mean. It is not that unlikely. All you have to go on are the words and whatever you know about the person sending the message. Words without tone of voice, body language, facial expressions, the speed of the message, and punctuation put you at a great disadvantage. The message is always more than just the words, but that is all that you have with a text, e-mail, or post. The other factors are missing.

Sometimes we try to compensate by using emojis, which can help, but it does not solve the problem. Your response may be received and interpreted differently. The potential for miscommunication and creating hard feelings is a real danger. If you are going to communicate through texts, make sure you slow down. Take some time to consider the text you received relative to the sender and their perspective. Take additional time to think about and reread your response before you hit the send button. These principles apply to and are equally important in e-mail conversations.

Emojis can help, but they do not solve the potential problems created as a result of a "words only" communication. Emojis are popular and used a great deal. In a survey conducted by Harris Poll and commissioned by GIF platform Tenor, 36 percent of millennials ages eighteen to thirty-four who use such "visual expressions" as emojis, GIFs, and stickers say those images better communicate their thoughts and feelings than words do.[1] Based on this survey, it would be helpful if we had a dictionary of emojis with specific definitions for each one. It would be helpful to have specific details as to the message each emoji conveys. This glossary or dictionary would help to minimize the many ways an emoji can be interpreted.

As of June 2018, it was reported that there are 2,823 different emojis. Each person interprets and uses emojis in different ways. There are multiple meanings for each emoji. Relying on emojis to help relay your message is potentially dangerous and, at best, relatively ineffective.

EFFECTIVE E-MAIL PRACTICES

As you slow down the conversation that is being transmitted through electronic devices it will be helpful to look at some guidelines for successful e-mail communications. E-mail communication is not likely to disappear anytime soon. It is estimated that the average worker spends thirteen hours each week on e-mails. Are e-mails the "conversations" of the twenty-first century? E-mails have their place, but they should never take the place of face-to-face communication and conversation.

E-mail can be an effective tool in sending a message to a group of people in various locations in an efficient way; however, it can also be ineffective if the sender is not thoughtful and careful in crafting the message. The following practices will assist you in developing an effective e-mail:

- Keep it short.
- List your recommendation/request early on.
- Do not use e-mail to avoid a tough conversation.

- Be careful about what you put in the e-mail.
- Never send an emotionally charged e-mail.
- Limit the number of "back and forth" e-mails.

Number one, keep it short. If it is more than four or five paragraphs, it is most likely a communication that would be handled much better through an actual conversation. Most individuals do not have an attention span that will allow them to read through the entire e-mail.

Number two, list your recommendations and/or requests early on in the e-mail. In other words, get to the point early so the receiver is not guessing about the purpose of the e-mail. It also assists in keeping the e-mail relatively short. If you have to use a lot of words leading up to your request or recommendation, there is probably a great deal of justifying or rationalization that needs to take place. If that is the case, then perhaps an actual conversation would be better.

Number three, never use an e-mail to avoid tough conversations. Difficult conversations cannot be handled through a one-sided e-mail. The difficult e-mail will elicit a response from the individual, which will cause you to respond, and the back and forth will continue. Deal with difficult situations through an actual conversation.

Number four, be careful about what you put in an e-mail. A good rule of thumb is to make sure there is nothing in the e-mail that will damage your reputation or character if it were forwarded to someone else either purposely or accidently. You need to consider that it may not be handled confidentially. If the information is confidential and personally sensitive, do not put it in an e-mail.

Number five, never send an emotionally charged e-mail. You can write it out, but then delete it. Sometimes it feels easier to write things in an e-mail that you would never say to a person face to face. Slow down, control your emotions, and think carefully before you hit that send button. If your emotions are running high, hit the delete button instead of the send button. You will be much better off in the long run.

Number six, limit the number of e-mails that go back and forth on the same subject. Let reasonableness be your guide. If the issue needs further clarification or is not resolved after three or four exchanges, it is time to pick up the phone or make a visit to have an actual conversation with the person.

These principles apply to or can be modified to apply to texting and posting on social media. The FBI is aware of many of the problems that posting can create. Recently they launched a #thinkbeforeyoupost campaign. The *FBI Chicago* has produced a public service announcement (PSA) relative to this campaign, warning social media users to strongly consider the ramifications and consequences of their messages before they are posted. The PSA includes the testimonial of a college student who posted a threat online. This individual suffered the ramifications of the post. This is a portion of the PSA transcript, in the words of the student:

> At the time, I just wasn't thinking. I used social media to vent. I wished I would have thought about effects of scaring people. I didn't mean for that to happen. People took it as a terrorist threat; the university got shut down; I got arrested by the FBI; and now, I don't know what my future looks like. It's not going away.[2]

There is no doubt there are limitations to e-mail communication. Susan serves as president of the board of directors for a nonprofit association serving clients from a fairly large region. The board is comprised of twelve members, and traditionally the members are local to the area where the nonprofit is headquartered. The individuals on the board do not fairly represent the wider region. The board has struggled with how to encourage individuals outside of the region surrounding the headquarters to serve on the board.

After one of the board members resigned, the board needed to appoint someone to fill the vacancy. It was Susan's recommendation to appoint Brad, an individual who had expressed interest in the past; however, Brad too was from the headquarters area. Susan polled the other officers, and the decision was made to include the appointment of Brad on the next agenda for action. Susan sent an e-mail indicating that the executive committee of the board was recommending Brad to fill the vacancy.

One of the board members immediately responded indicating their support of Brad based on prior interactions with him. One of the other board members indicated that although he did not have an issue with Brad, he believed that the board should be actively pursuing candidates from other regions. Susan's initial emotion was not very positive because she knew the board had held this very discussion many times in the past and discussed how virtually impossible it was to get individuals from outside the region who were qualified and had an interest in serving. Susan immediately jumped to the thought that the board member was just being difficult.

Susan decided to slow down and pause for a minute. As she thought about it, she felt that, instead of responding in an e-mail, she should just call this board member. It was not something she really wanted to do, but she did feel it was the right thing to do.

Susan waited to get her emotions further in check, but in the meantime, there was a follow-up e-mail from the same board member again reiterating his position. At that point, Susan needed to respond by e-mail so that the entire board would be aware of her rationale. If she simply called him and explained, the rest of the board would not know she had responded and would not be privy to her rationale for taking a different approach.

So, Susan carefully crafted an e-mail response and sent it out to the entire board. She then picked up the phone and called the individual, and listened to him explain verbally his concern. She also asked for his help in identifying individuals outside of the immediate area. She decided to elicit his help as a way of demonstrating that she valued his concerns. Susan then explained over the phone her rationale. She again acknowledged his position and expressed what she believed to be the challenges that it imposed. The two of them had a great conversation.

At the board meeting, Susan was able to let the board know about the phone conversation the two of them had. The result was that the vacancy was filled with the recommended candidate by a unanimous vote. The point is, Susan slowed down the conversation, got her emotions in check, and developed a plan that resulted in a win–win situation. After the meeting, the board member was able to reach out to an individual outside of the area, and that person expressed interest in serving on the board. The successful outcome of this situation demonstrates the benefit of slowing down, controlling emotions, and respecting differences.

If it is impossible to have a face-to-face meeting, at least make a phone call. Although body language will be missing, you will at least be able to ascertain tonality, rate of speech, pitch, and volume. In addition, you have the advantage of immediate feedback so that you can have a back-and-forth conversation.

Another example of slowing down that had a positive outcome was reported by *NBC News*. The story was of a comedian who, as a part of his comedic routine, said some things that were negative toward President Trump. Someone who heard the statements took exception to the derogatory remarks and tweeted a not-so-nice message about the comedian. (This particular comedian was in a certain movie where the character he played ended up dying.) The tweet directed at the comedian essentially said, "I liked you better in the movie where you died."

The comedian was justifiably angry and upset at such a comment. Instead of getting in a tweet war with the man, he slowed down and carefully thought about the situation. He decided to check the individual out through social media. This is perhaps one of the positives of social media. Through something as simple as social media, he was able to understand a bit more about the individual's background. The comedian was taking a positive approach to consider the other person's perspective. He was proactively allowing for differences.

What he discovered through his research was that the man was having some major medical issues and struggling with the financial means to address them. So there was not only great stress related to his medical condition, but also the added anxiety of wondering where the money would come from to pay his medical bills.

Having a new perspective, the comedian decided to let the comment go and set up a GoFundMe account to help with the man's medical bills. As a result, the comedian and this individual have been in communication through social media and developed quite a positive relationship. The conversation creates the relationship. Imagine the outcome if the comedian had returned the initial tweet with a defensive response. The outcome would have been totally different.

SUMMARY

Slowing down can make a big difference in the outcomes of difficult situations—not just a difference, a big difference, potentially as different as night and day. Do not look at the slower pace as a waste of time. Time spent in preparation before the conversation will be invaluable. Slowing down during the actual conversation will pay dividends in the long term. Not spending the time can derail the process and result in many unintended consequences. Slowing down after the interaction and the conversation is just as important. Reflecting on the interaction and the outcome will be helpful in handling future situations. The importance of reflection is covered in chapter 9.

CHAPTER 8 RECAP

- Slowing down before the conversation means that you take the time to think about the desired outcome and then develop a plan as to how you are going to accomplish it. Considering the other person's perspective is an important preconversation aspect of planning.
- During the conversation, slow down to make sure you are truly adhering to the principles of an effective and meaningful conversation. Slow down to make sure you are allowing the other person enough time to adequately express themselves.
- Make sure you slow down the response. Be sure your emotions are in check and that you carefully choose your words.
- Slowing down is crucial when communicating through e-mail and texts. There are six practices for effective e-mailing: 1) Keep it short; 2) list your recommendations and requests early on in the e-mail; 3) never use e-mail to avoid tough conversations; 4) be careful about what you put in an e-mail, as it could easily be forwarded to someone else without you knowing; 5) never send an emotionally charged e-mail; and 6) limit the number of e-mails that go back on forth on the same subject.
- Slow down what you are posting on social media sites. Posting on social media can be dangerous unless you slow down and carefully consider what you are about to post. What are the ramifications? Have you consid-

ered that certain people might misinterpret it or be offended? If you have any reservations at all or are emotionally charged, hit the delete button, not the send button.

NOTES

1. Katy Steinmetz, "Forget Words, a Lot of Millennials Say GIFs and Emojis Communicate Their Thoughts Better Than English," *Time*, June 27, 2017. Accessed June 25, 2019, https://time.com/4834112/millennials-gifs-emojis/.

2. "Think before You Post PSA," FBI Chicago, n.d. Accessed June 25, 2019, https://www.fbi.gov/video-repository/think-before-you-post-psa.mp4/view.

Chapter Nine

Reflect

> Without reflection, we go blindly on our way, creating more unintended consequences, and failing to achieve anything useful.
> —Margaret J. Wheatley

You may be wondering what a chapter on reflection is doing in a book about words and conversation. Let us first look at the definition of reflection as it might relate to challenging situations and conversations. There are many different definitions for reflection according to *Merriam-Webster*. To be exact, there are nine different meanings for reflection. For our purposes here, we are going to look at definitions six and seven. Definition number six states, "Reflection is a thought, idea, or opinion formed or a remark made as a result of meditation." Definition number seven states, "Reflection is the consideration of some subject matter, idea, or purpose." The two definitions can be combined to highlight the idea that reflection includes the concepts of meditation, as well as thoughtful consideration of thoughts, actions, words, intentions, and ideas.

As a practice, reflection is a way to think about a prior occurrence. It is a way to replay the scenario in your head, to critique and evaluate the process and the outcome. The outcome is important, but so is the process. Thoughtfully evaluating both the process and the outcome will be helpful in guiding future approaches and the handling of future situations.

MEDITATION

To understand what meaningful reflection is, let us take a look at the thoughts and beliefs surrounding meditation. Meditation is not a new concept. It is an ancient practice that is believed to have originated in India several thousand years BCE (Before Common Era). It quickly became a part of many religions throughout the world.

While meditation is not unique to Buddhism, it is something that holds deep importance in Buddhist teachings. The happy life is based on this core concept. Buddhists are taught that there are five ways to maintain a happy life. All five are closely tied to reflection and meditation. The five methods are as follows:

1. Let go; leave behind obstacles to joy and happiness.
2. Invite positive seeds; think about the positive.
3. Practice mindfulness-based joy, the practice of mindful breathing.
4. Concentrate; stay in the present moment.
5. Gain insight—see what is; clarity that liberates from negative feelings.

In Christianity, the Bible contains many verses that reference the importance of careful thought, reflection, and meditation. One such verse is found in the book of Philippians, chapter 4, verses 8 and 9:

> Summing it all up, friends, I'd say you'll do best by filling your minds and meditating on things true, noble, reputable, authentic, compelling, gracious—the best, not the worst; the beautiful, not the ugly; things to praise, not things to curse. Put into practice what you learned from me, what you heard and saw and realized. Do that, and God, who makes everything work together, will work you into his most excellent harmonies. [The Message translation]

Meditation and reflection imply quiet time and time alone. Most of us are not very good at this. Our society has become fast paced, loud, noisy, and crowded. We are overstimulated with videos, music, texts, and a myriad of other types of technology distractions. We rarely, if ever, take the time to just sit quietly without some kind of noise or interference. In fact, if you are quiet or somewhere off by yourself you may be viewed as weird.

We are on the phone, sending or receiving texts, watching shows and movies, and reading or sending e-mails. We are most likely listening to a variety of genres of music through earbuds that are stuffed in our ears. Granted, the right kind of instrumental music may actually enhance reflection and meditation, especially if it is blocking out external noise. Instrumental music is suggested since the lyrics of a song may distract you from a dedicated thought process.

Find a good time and place to reflect. If you travel, the airplane can be a great place to spend time in reflection. You are confined to a specific seat in a plane and can use that time for thoughtful reflection. To maintain focus, it may be helpful to write down your thoughts on paper or type them onto a tablet or laptop. You will most likely notice that most other passengers on the plane have headphones on and are connected to their electronic device. They may be watching movies, the latest Netflix series, or a myriad of other things. Quite frankly, travel used to be a great way to have conversations and get to know people sitting near or next to you. Now the norm seems to be to get to your seat and immediately hook yourself up with headphones and some form of entertainment. Since that is the case, the plane ride can be very conducive to reflective practices. It is generally quiet, and for the most part you are confined to your seat.

There are many other great places to practice reflection. It may be your favorite spot at a nearby park, the beach, next to a mountain stream, or in the comfort of your own home. Wherever it is, find a spot and take some time to reflect.

Why You Should Reflect or Meditate

There are several reasons to take the time for thoughtful reflection or meditation. One of them is a tangible health benefit. A study conducted by the University of California Davis found that people who regularly practice meditation have higher levels of telomerase, the enzyme responsible for lengthening the telomeres at the ends of your chromosomes, which positively affect aging.[1] Another study found that cancer patients who combined meditation with other healthy lifestyle changes during a span of several years were able to lengthen their telomeres.[2] Meditation is also a good way to manage stress and blood pressure, which can prevent a number of other diseases caused by stress.

Aside from the physical benefits, there are other benefits as well. It is helpful to reflect on your actions. Thoughtfully consider the results of your interactions and conversations with others. Was there a successful outcome? Was there a more effective way to deal with the situation? Reflection informs your future practice. It assists you in improving your approach. It helps you grow and become a better version of yourself.

MINDFULNESS

Closely related to meditation and reflection is the concept of mindfulness. As people realize that participating in a fast paced, highly stimulating society is creating stress, anxiety, and other related health issues, there has been a move toward mindfulness. Mindfulness is not a new idea but it is currently trendy and skyrocketing in popularity.

According to Dr. Jon Kabat-Zinn, professor of medicine emeritus from the University of Massachusetts, mindfulness is defined as "paying attention in a particular way: on purpose, in the present moment and non-judgmentally."[3] Practicing mindfulness has been proven to reduce anxiety, depression, and pain. Two of the major types of mindfulness are meditation and yoga.

Perhaps as we get deeper into social media and experience less and less person-to-person interaction, there will be an increased resurgence and need for the ideas surrounding mindfulness. As more and more individuals are diagnosed with anxiety and depression-related disorders, the idea of mindfulness will increasingly become a much-needed practice. *Psychology Today* reports that anxiety and depression among teens and young adults has increased substantially in the United States over the past five years.[4] Based on societal pressures and the impact of social media, that trend is unlikely to get any better. There is a real need to employ the concepts of mindfulness, reflection, and meditation.

REFLECTION

Reviewing the concepts of meditation and mindfulness is helpful in laying the groundwork for reflection. Some of the principles of meditation and mindfulness are similar to the ideas of reflection in the context of this book.

Self-reflection is an important leadership quality. Roshan Thiran, CEO of Leaderonomics Group, was recently asked an interesting question. If he could have just one leadership quality that would be guaranteed to remain constant, what would it be? After much thought, his response was that the leadership quality that is at the heart of effective leadership is self-reflection. His rationale for this choice was that everything begins with knowing what you are doing, why you are doing it, and how you are doing it.[5]

Self-reflection is an important quality for everyone whether you consider yourself a leader or not. Self-reflection is an important quality of a self-secure and confident individual. There is a maturity that develops from self-reflection. It is an important part of growing and improving one's own self.

Why We Don't Reflect

Self-reflection can be painful. It forces us to come to grips with our words, actions, or intentions that may not have been appropriate or effective. It is difficult to be critical of ourselves. Instead of facing our weaknesses, inabilities, or other shortcomings head-on, we would rather make excuses for them.

Facing those negativities head-on means we need to do something with them. We may need to retrace our steps and make a wrong right. We may need to apologize. It may be a matter of awareness for the next time we are faced with a similar situation. None of us like to face our weaknesses or deal with our actions that may have been wrong. We certainly do not like to admit we were wrong to others.

There is a reason that so much attention has been given to the words "I'm sorry" and the importance of forgiveness. Part of forgiveness is admitting we were wrong. A major part of forgiveness is reflecting on how we can avoid making the same mistake again.

Effective self-reflection requires us to be brutally honest with ourselves. It should not be done in a way where we beat ourselves up, but it should be done in a way that we uncover and come face-to-face with uncomfortable truths.

Why You Should Reflect

We can certainly influence other people's behavior, but we cannot control it. The only thing we can control is ourselves. Self-reflection is helpful for self-improvement and overall personal growth and development. It helps in developing us as a person who is self-confident without being brash or arrogant. It develops a security in knowing who we are. The goal is to strive for a healthy attitude and balance between the acceptance of oneself while still searching for ways to improve oneself—being comfortable but not complacent, always looking for ways to develop and get better.

Reflection gives your brain an opportunity to rest from the craziness of the world. We need a break from the constant mental stress of life and its challenges. Pausing to sort out your observations and experiences provides an opportunity to create learning, which then translates into future actions. This is crucial to ongoing growth and development.

Jennifer Porter, managing partner of the Boda Group, discusses the importance of making time for self-reflection in an article that appeared in the *Harvard Business Review*. Research conducted by Giada Di Stefano, Francesca Gino, Gary Pisano, and Bradley Staats in call centers demonstrated that employees who spent fifteen minutes at the end of the day reflecting about lessons learned performed 23 percent better after ten days than those who did not reflect. Also writes Porter, "A study of UK commuters found a similar result when those who were prompted to use their commute to think about and plan for their day were happier, more productive, and less burned out than people who didn't."[6]

One of the jobs Sean had several years ago required a daily commute of forty miles each way. It typically took an hour each way. On the way to work, he used the time to think about the upcoming events of his day. On the way home he spent the time reflecting on the day's happenings—evaluating, critiquing, and figuring out what he personally could have done to make it a better day for not only himself, but also others.

Sean was often encouraged by others to use the commute time to listen to audio books, but he resisted using the time in that way because he believed in the importance of reflection. For Sean, the ride was the perfect time for a thoughtful review of the upcoming day or the completed workday. He knew it was unlikely that he would discipline himself enough to carve out other time in the day for self-reflection. Sean knew that self-reflection is important. He knew it was essential to find the time in his daily routine even if was only for a few minutes a day to start. He realized that if you continue to practice reflection for a period of time, it will become a regular habit.

At that same job, Sean was part of a team that was effective, productive, and enjoyable. Sean enjoyed running, and one of the team members was also a runner. At the end of most workdays they would go for a run along the canal. It was a great time to decompress and reflect. Because of the valued and trusting relationship that existed between the two of them, they were able to provide feedback to one another on work and personal life events that provided incredibly useful information for their own self-improvement.

Sean could count on his running mate and work colleague to give honest feedback from his perspective. They had more differences than things in common, which made the feedback even more valuable. Sean knew that feedback from a different frame of reference is important and useful. Sometimes the feedback was difficult to hear, but Sean knew it was always offered in the spirit of friendship and his own betterment.

Reflection Related to Challenging Conversations

In the early to mid-1900s, which were arguably less hectic times, people took more time to reflect. It was not a conscious deliberate practice, it just happened naturally and organically. People sat on porches with family and neighborhood friends talking about the issues of life. The conversations were a chance for everyone to offer their opinion, advice, and general feedback. The porch was a safe space. It was a natural and organic way to be challenged in your thinking. The discussion enabled people to see things differently and grow and mature. There were understandably a fair amount of disagreements and perhaps difficult conversations, but in the end it created and fostered meaningful relationships. Children were exposed to and then included in these "porch chats" as they grew up. It was modeled for them, and so they became comfortable with courageous conversations.

Today's environment is quite different. We have moved away from that kind of quality time. We are so busy running from event to event that we rarely take the time to just sit and talk about life. We do not take the time to just slow down and listen.

Reflection after a Difficult Interaction or Conversation

Reflection is often viewed as a waste of time. There is so much to do, so much on one's to-do list. Sitting quietly is seen as odd. If you have seen someone sitting quietly by themselves you may have thought, "Is there something wrong?" Imagine that your boss walks into your office where you are sitting quietly in thoughtful consideration. He or she asks you what you are doing. Your response is, "I'm reflecting." This statement might be greeted with the response, "Get back to work."

Unfortunately, reflection is not common practice. Think about the way we communicate through texting. In the world of fast-paced texts we rarely think about the impact of our words. We do not take the time to reflect on the message we send or the impact it may have had. We rarely get feedback, and, if there is any, it comes in the form of a text response or an emoji.

As shared in an earlier chapter, a 2017 survey of millennials reflected that 36 percent of them believe that emojis are more important than words.[7] That is interesting but not all that shocking. It is, however, a bit scary. How many different interpretations are there for each emoji? If you asked ten different people to describe one particular emoji, you would get ten different and unique descriptions and meanings.

Timing

To maximize the meaningfulness and benefit of the reflection it needs to be done as soon as possible after the interaction or conversation. Reflecting immediately thereafter assures that the conversation or interaction is still fresh in your mind. If you are unable to spend the necessary time after the event, take a limited amount of time to at least make some notes. The notes should highlight the aspects of the conversation that were most impactful or important. You will be able to refresh your memory with the notes when you finally have the time to reflect. Do not put it off. Do it as soon as possible.

Best Reflection Practices

If you were the only other person in the conversation, you will have to reflect on your own. The following are some questions you might ask yourself:

- Did I adhere to the principles of an effective conversation?
- Was the timing of the conversation appropriate?
- Was the outcome as expected?
- Is there a need to follow up with the individual?
- How could I have planned better for this conversation?
- Did I adhere to the proposed plan for this conversation?
- Is there something I could have handled more effectively or successfully?

If there was someone else with you in the conversation, you will most likely be able to get valuable feedback. Those methods will be discussed in the feedback section in this chapter.

One of the questions you should ask yourself during reflection is whether or not there is a need to follow up with the individual you had the conversation with. Following up may not always be necessary or appropriate, but you should always give careful consideration to that possibility. In most cases, it is good to follow up with the individual, especially if it is a difficult situation or circumstance. Just as you are reflecting and thinking about the conversation, the other party is most likely doing the same thing. You may determine that you did not say something that you should have or that you said something wrong. The other party may be contemplating the same thing or something similar.

Following up not only allows either party to correct or add anything additional, but also shows that you truly care about the individual. You are checking in on them. You care about them and the impact of the conversation.

Many times, the second conversation is much better than the original. Both parties have had a chance to process the interaction. Follow up right away, as appropriate, so that any negative feelings or ramifications from the conversation are not aggravated. If you allow too much time to transpire, you run the risk that the individual will share with colleagues or family members. These colleagues or family members may have a negative attitude toward you or the organization. Allowing too much time sets up the potential for others to influence the individual in a not so positive way.

Feedback

Feedback is simply getting information and reactions to a situation based on a participating individual's reflection. It is asking someone else to tell you what their reflection on the situation has revealed. The best and most useful feedback will come from someone you have a trusting relationship with, someone who is interested in your success and personal growth.

If there was someone in the conversation with you, their input and feedback may be very helpful. To get that feedback you will need to ask specific and targeted questions. You will not get useful feedback by simply asking them to give you feedback. You will need to be more specific or you will most likely get a generic, nonuseful response. Some questions you can ask are listed here:

- I feel like I may not have given them enough time to express their concerns. Is that the way you see it?
- I got frustrated when they blamed someone else for their behavior and did not accept responsibility. Did my body language and tone reflect my frustration?
- When I stated the consequences of their action, what was your sense of how they reacted? Was there a better way I could have stated the ramifications that would have been more effective?

Ask questions that are specific to the situation and conversation. See if they agree with your assessment of the conversation based on your own reflections.

Former Harvard Business professor David Maister is quoted as saying, "If you are going to ask for feedback, be ready to change."[8] The feedback can be helpful and useful but difficult to hear. You may be able to follow up and correct something that may have gone wrong. At the very least, you will be able to improve your conversation skills so that next time you have a better experience and result.

Reflection and feedback allow you to correct wrong thoughts or actions and learn from them so you are more productive the next time. It is always good to reflect on your words, actions, and intentions. As you reflect on their appropriateness and effectiveness in the situation, make sure that they are in alignment. Oftentimes the words we use are not aligned with our intentions and our actions are not aligned with the words or intentions. We all remember the saying, "Do as I say, not as I do." We need to strive for a unified message. The words and actions should be aligned with our intentions.

SUMMARY

Reflection is such an important concept. It is essential for so many different aspects of life. It is crucial to effective leadership. A leader who is able to reflect on his or her practices and honestly assess the success and value of those practices is a leader who is looking to continuously improve. It is tough to look at one's own faults and failures, but absent an honest assessment of our actions, we will continue to repeat the mistakes of the past. It takes a strong and confident individual to be able to honestly look in the mirror and realize that there are changes to be made—changes that may require us to engage in some tough and challenging activities.

Reflection is important as we consider conversational principles. We need to reflect on every difficult and crucial conversation to determine if we adhered to the principles, if we could have handled things differently, and if the results of the conversation were positive. If we do not reflect inwardly and honestly, we will not be in a position to improve our practice. We need to be in the business of improving our leadership, our relationships, and our overall communication. Remember, if you are not growing, you are dying. Lou Holtz said it this way: "In this world you are either growing or you are dying, so get in motion and grow."

CHAPTER 9 RECAP

- Reflection is important. Make time for it.
- Reflect on your words, actions, and intentions.

- Reflection and meditation reduce stress and increase health and happiness.
- Reflection is step one, and step two is taking action based on the results of your reflection.
- Honest reflection requires taking a hard look and confronting the difficult stuff.
- Reflection, when possible, should include feedback from trusted colleagues and friends.

NOTES

1. Andy Fell, "Positive Psychological Changes from Meditation Training Linked to Cellular Health," University of California Davis, November 3, 2010. Accessed July 18, 2019, https://www.ucdavis.edu/news/positive-psychological-changes-meditation-training-linked-cellular-health/.

2. Elizabeth Fernandez, "Lifestyle Changes May Lengthen Telomeres, a Measure of Cell Aging," University of California San Francisco, September 16, 2013. Accessed July 18, 2018, https://www.ucsf.edu/news/2013/09/108886/lifestyle-changes-may-lengthen-telomeres-measure-cell-aging.

3. Jon Kabat-Zinn, quoted in Mindful Staff, "Jon Kabat-Zinn: Defining Mindfulness: What Is Mindfulness? The Founder of Mindfulness-Based Stress Reduction Explains," Mindful, January 11, 2017. Accessed July 19, 2019, https://www.mindful.org/jon-kabat-zinn-defining-mindfulness/.

4. Scott M. Stanley, "Young and Cueless: Thinking about the Big Rise in Anxiety," *Psychology Today*, November 7, 2017. Accessed July 19, 2019, https://www.psychologytoday.com/us/blog/sliding-vs-deciding/201711/young-and-cueless-thinking-about-the-big-rise-in-anxiety.

5. Roshan Thiran, "To Become an Effective Leader, You Need to Practice Self-Reflection," Leaderonomics, August 29, 2017. Accessed July 18, 2019, https://leaderonomics.com/leadership/practise-self-reflection.

6. Jennifer Porter, "Why You Should Make Time for Self-Reflection (Even if You Hate Doing It)," *Harvard Business Review*, March 21, 2017. Accessed June 25, 2019, https://hbr.org/2017/03/why-you-should-make-time-for-self-reflection-even-if-you-hate-doing-it.

7. Katy Steinmetz, "Forget Words, a Lot of Millennials Say GIFs and Emojis Communicate Their Thoughts Better Than English," *Time*, June 27, 2017. Accessed June 25, 2019, https://time.com/4834112/millennials-gifs-emojis/.

8. David Meister, "Getting Good at Feedback," *David Meister* (blog), July 6, 2006, davidmeister.com.

Chapter Ten

Create the Win–Win

> The Law of Win–Win says let's not do it your way or my way, let's do it the best way.
>
> —Greg Anderson

Perhaps win–win is not the best label or term to capture the essence of this final conversational principle. It is a buzzword that carries many different meanings and connotations. In general, for purposes here, think of it in terms of a result that is positive for both parties involved in the conversation, interaction, or negotiation. In many situations the conversation is a negotiation of sorts. The principles of conversation are certainly applicable to negotiation situations.

Win–win conjures up the idea of sports, and using the term *win* implies that someone loses. In fact, practically speaking, there is no win–win in sports. One person or team wins and the other person or team loses. Sometimes the result of the competition is a tie. In the case of a tie, no one feels really good about it because there is no winner or loser. No one was victorious.

Win–win also implies a competition or rivalry and everything that comes along with competing. It invokes such statements as, "Put your game face on" or "We are in it to win it." Some competitors are "cutthroat." Preparations for the competition are focused on having every advantage against the competitor.

This is not the way to use win–win when it comes to challenging conversations or any conversation for that matter. Win–win is described on Wikipedia as, "All participants can profit from the solution in one way or another." In conflict resolution, win–win is aimed at accommodating every participant.

Many businesses are adopting a win–win type of business model. Sometimes it is referred to as "profit for purpose." Traditionally, businesses have been focused on a relatively one-sided approach. The goal was to acquire as much profit as possible. Their goal was to make sure the shareholders "win." "Profit for purposes" is a new way of thinking. Profit is generated to provide resources for enhanced mission work, increasing organizational performance and sustainability, as well as to create new opportunities to help clients. This approach is certainly a focus on a more mutually beneficial relationship between the business, the client, and outside mission-type work. It is the convergence of doing business and doing good.

Win–win, as used here for the purposes of a challenging conversation, is not the same as the concept of gamesmanship. Gamesmanship is the idea of pushing the rules to the limit to gain a serious advantage. You may be in a position of power and therefore have the authority to push the limits of the rules and have full advantage. The idea of win–win is different. You need to do your best to even the playing field, make sure that both sides have the same rules and that they are followed and enforced equally.

Win–win is not about manipulation. Making the other party feel like they won may seem to work for a bit, but eventually they will figure out that they have been manipulated. Manipulation is not a good approach. It does not value and respect the other individual. Manipulation may seem like a quick, easy fix to put the problem behind you, but eventually it will surface again. When it does, you will be in a worse position because you have ruined any bit of trust that may have been initially gained.

Playing hardball through gamesmanship and manipulation may lead to reprisals and retaliation at some future date. The losing party may decide to be uncooperative in fulfilling their part of the deal. Tricks, pushing the limits, and manipulation undermines trust and damages any hope for teamwork.

DEVELOP STANDARDS OF CONDUCT

To work toward a mutually agreeable resolution to the difficult conversation, it is good to agree on some standards of conduct for the conversation. This is especially important and helpful if it is a conversation that lends itself to a negotiation. There are times when the conversation is more defined and restrictive. For example, if it is an employee discipline situation you may have to set the standards of conduct whether they agree to them or not. Whatever the specific situation, it is a good idea to develop standards of conduct.

Even if you do not discuss it with the other party, your acknowledgment of the standards will help. You cannot control their behavior, you can only control yours. If the conversation is conducive to discussing the standards, that would certainly be an advantage as you work toward a successful outcome. Good standards to adopt include the following:

- Respect and care for the other party.
- Adhere to the principles of good conversation.
- Agree to keep the conversation going.
- Summarize at the end of each meeting.

Respect and Care for the Other Party

The most important and overarching standard of conduct is valuing and respecting the individual involved in the conversation. You need to start with care and respect for the other person. The idea is that you truly want the best for them. Even if you do not respect their actions or like their personality, for the purposes of a successful conversation you need to act in a way that is respectful of who they are. You need to show them that you care about them as a person.

Adhere to the Principles of Good Conversation

To work toward a mutually beneficial agreement through the conversation, make sure you acknowledge and embrace the concepts of good conversation as outlined in this book. Be careful with the words you choose. Thoughtfully consider the way those words may be interpreted by the person on the receiving end. It does not matter what you think they mean or what you intend them to mean, it is all about what those words mean to that person and how they interpret them. You certainly are not able to read their mind, but you can carefully consider how they may react.

Do your best to control your emotions. This is important before the conversation and at all times during the conversation, and it is equally important after the conversation is over. This is not easy, but it will go a long way in assuring a meaningful interaction.

Creating that safe space is so important. Do everything you can to make the conversation comfortable for the other individual. If you are in a position of authority, you may have to exaggerate this effort to provide an environment that is free of tension and stress.

When you speak, do so with heartfelt care and thoughtful consideration. Through your words and actions show them that you care about them as a person. Even if the feeling is not mutual, you can make the effort to value and honor them. It is about basic respect. Everyone deserves an initial extension of that decency.

Listen with your ears, mind, and heart. Hearing and listening to them sounds easy initially; however, active listening involves the idea of being all in. You are engaged in the conversation and acknowledging, clarifying, and questioning throughout the conversation.

Keep your mental models in check. Mental models are the perceptions you have about people. They make it difficult to keep an open mind. Your mental models are restrictive and make unfair assumptions based on your own experiences and perceptions. Allow for differences—differences in belief systems, opinions, values, and desired outcomes. Do not let the differences cloud the rationality and reasonableness of your desired outcome.

Slow down as you engage in the conversation. Seeking that win–win may take time. It will be worth the extra time. Rushing the process may seem like an efficient and time-saving approach, but in the end it will come at a cost.

Finally, remember to reflect. As you are engaged in conversation remember to thoughtfully think about the desired outcome. Think about how the other party is reacting. Think about how you may need to adjust your approach based on their verbal and nonverbal responses. After the conversation, take the time to assess whether the outcome was truly a win–win result.

Agree to Keep the Conversation Going

Make a commitment to keep working on the issue until you reach a successful conclusion. Regardless of the issues and emotions, agree that you will continue to talk. At times it may feel like you have reached an impasse. If so, take a break. You might only need a few minutes or an hour, a day, or a week. Sometimes all you need is a few minutes, just enough time to walk away, take a deep breath, and remind yourself of the desired win–win outcome. Whatever time period is appropriate, make sure you commit to setting up a follow-up meeting. The extra time will allow you to cool off, get additional information, and put things in perspective. It will allow the other party to do the same. Most importantly, make sure you pick a time to get together again so that you keep the dialogue going.

Summarize at the End of Each Meeting

Depending on the complexity and importance of the meeting, you may want to take notes. At the very least make sure you summarize the action items from the meeting. It is always a good idea to restate what both parties have agreed to. If there were any items that still seem to be sticking points, it is good to restate them as well. Finally, talk about next steps and set a follow-up meeting date. Do not leave the meeting without a follow-up meeting scheduled. Even if you have to reschedule it later, it is better to commit to a date before you part ways. Even if you feel that all the issues have been addressed and resolved, it is a good idea to get together again to assess the situation. It will also help to continue the development of the relationship.

STRATEGIES TO REACH WIN–WIN

The overarching strategy to achieve a win–win result is to adhere to the principles of a good conversation, as outlined in the previous chapters. Looking for a win–win is applicable to every conversation in some ways, but is most important when it comes to those difficult and challenging situations where a conversation is necessary to resolve a problematic situation. The following are some specific steps that can be taken to increase the chances for a successful outcome:

- Agree to standards of conduct.
- Focus on the issue.
- Figure out where they are.
- Think outside the box.
- Know your fallback position.

Agree to Standards of Conduct

It is a good practice to develop some ground rules for the conversation. Create the ground rules prior to the interaction and then review them with the other party. Work toward agreement. You may not be able to get total agreement, but it will certainly be worth the effort. This will be helpful to the conversation.

Focus on the Issue

If it is a challenging conversation it will most likely be emotionally charged. Once you realize that, make sure you put your emotions in check. You will not be able to control the other party's emotions, but your calm approach will help to diffuse whatever emotion they are exhibiting. If you react in a negatively emotional way it will only "fuel their fire."

Keep the focus of the conversation on the issue at hand. It is easy to get sidetracked and end up on other issues. There may be issues that surface as a result of the emotions that are running high based on the situation. The other party may want to derail the conversation for obvious reasons. Make sure you do not fall into that trap. Keep your calm and always bring the conversation back to the issues at hand.

If the other party appears to be unreasonable and is positioning themselves to be unwavering and rigid, it will be easy for you to get caught up in that. Resist the desire to respond to everything they are saying. If you do, it will end up being a vicious cycle. When that happens, remind yourself to redirect the conversation back to the issue at hand. You may want to offer to put those issues in a "parking lot" until the key issue is resolved. It simply means that you are acknowledging the issue and offering to "park" the issue for a later discussion. You are temporarily suspending that matter but not ignoring it.

Make sure you are clear as to what the focus of the conversation is. If you are not clear, it will obviously be difficult to steer the conversation back to the main problem if you are unsure as to exactly what it is. Make sure you thoughtfully consider this before you enter the conversation. It is also helpful to decide what you want from the conversation. You may not get everything you want. If you do get what you want, do not get greedy and ask for more based on the way they are acting and reacting during the meeting. Again, guard against the emotional approach and reaction. Be reasonable and rational.

Related to focusing on the issues is providing any appropriate education on the matter to the other party. It may be that the other party does not fully understand the particular concern. If you are negotiating an employment contract, one of the issues in reaching agreement might be the cost of the agreement related to employee benefits. You can continually state how expensive the benefits are and that the organization cannot afford to pay that level of benefits.

It is much more beneficial if you can help the individual understand the cost of the benefit. Explain the factors that are driving the cost. Share with them the history of the expense of this particular benefit. Provide comparative data as to what other organizations are providing to their employees. The individual may still want what they want, but at least you have done your part to share the impact. It will go a long way toward building a trusting relationship, which is so important.

Figure Out Where They Are

Understanding who they are and what they want will go a long way in reaching a mutually agreeable solution. This will not be easy, especially if you do not have much of an existing relationship with this individual. If your interactions have been limited you will be at a slight disadvantage.

This concept is, in large part, related to role reversal. You are trying to figure out what the other person is thinking and feeling. If you were in their shoes, how would you feel? It is about trying to figure out what the picture is in their head. You want to try to get to the crux of their issues. Consider what they want from the conversation.

Trying to determine their strategy is important. Are they taking a hard-line approach because they fear being taken advantage of? Are they asking for a lot more than they really want just so that you can "meet them in the middle"?

It will be helpful if you can assess whether their stated objective is what they really want. They may think that is what they want, but it may not be best for them. You can listen and then help them understand the ramifications of what they are asking for and guide them toward a different solution that will be better for them in the end.

As an example, consider the difficult conversation with an employee who is not performing satisfactory work. Their stated objective may be that they want to keep their job. If they are unhappy and stressed because of the job, you may be able to help them see things in a different way. Share with them the idea of finding work that they have a passion for and where their abilities lie. This would be a great service to them. Finding a place where they "fit in" will enhance the quality of their life.

Help them see past their current bad situation toward a brighter future. Help them discover their strengths as you see them. Help them realize that a more fulfilling and satisfying job will pay great dividends outside of the workplace. Work does not have to be a struggle. Job stress is not healthy. Helping them see the value of another placement will be good for them and for you (the employer) as well.

The ease or difficulty with which you are able to accomplish this will be based in part on the kind of relationship you have with the individual. Is it a trusting relationship based on a positive past history? If so, you have an advantage. Are they able to trust that you have their best interest at heart? It might be helpful to state the obvious, that you are looking out for the best interest of the organization but are doing so with their well-being as a crucial component as well.

To a great extent it really comes down to trust. You cannot make them trust you, but you can do your best to extend trust to them. You do not want to be foolish, but extending some bit of trust has limited risk. Extending that trust can pay great dividends. Show them through your words and actions that they can trust you.

Think Outside the Box

Be aware of and guard against limited thinking. There are countless solutions to any problem. Do not be restricted to traditional solutions. Do not be restricted to solutions that you have developed without input from anyone else.

Brainstorming is a technique used to generate a solution to a problem or issue. Those involved in the brainstorming activity spontaneously produce a list of ideas. The key is spontaneous. The ideas are not developed and have not been "thought through." The idea is to stimulate thinking and play off the ideas generated by others in the group.

Brainstorming can help in finding unique and innovative solutions. Remember, the only rule to brainstorming is that there are no ridiculous suggestions. The space should be free from judgment. There is no right or wrong. In fact, every idea is valid and worthy of consideration. The discussion generated from some of the craziest ideas may lead to a viable solution. The more "out-of-the-box" ideas that are generated, the better off you will be.

To stimulate out-of-the-box thinking it may be helpful to include others in the conversation. Someone who is not as close to the situation may be able to offer some insight or alternate solutions to the situation at hand.

One other opportunity to encourage out-of-the-box thinking is to take a break from the conversation. Allow some time to sit back and reflect. Do your best to think through the situation. Sometimes when you are removed from the intense focus and allow separation and distance from the conversation, it allows for some thoughtful consideration that may result in alternative solutions.

Know Your Fallback Position

Know what you are willing to accept as an outcome. What is the minimum you need to leave satisfied that you have reached a good solution? What are the things that are nonnegotiable? Try to limit the nonnegotiable list to the extent possible. Sometimes that is not possible, but you should make a concerted effort to limit that list. Imagine the difficulty if both parties have the same nonnegotiables from opposite standpoints.

For example, it might be a difficult conversation about poor job performance and continued employment. If you are the initiator of the conversation as the individual's supervisor, your nonnegotiable might be that the person must resign from their position. Their nonnegotiable may be that they have to leave the conversation still having a job. If it is a union situation you may not even have the authority or power to achieve your nonnegotiable.

The bottom line is that even though you may have the power to make your nonnegotiable happen, it is still more productive to let go of your nonnegotiable for a time to see if there is another solution. In other words, enter the conversation with an open mind. Granted, there will be times when the situation is so egregious that there truly may be no other option. There is still no danger in having a conversation to enhance your understanding of the circumstances from their standpoint.

In the case of a conversation about poor job performance, keep in mind the desire for a win–win result. Ask them how they think things are going with their job performance. Have them offer an honest assessment of the execution of their job functions. Ask for evidence of that assessment. Are they getting positive feedback from colleagues, clients, or customers? Inquire about the challenges they are facing in performing the work. Question their level of stress and happiness in the position. Probe a bit about what you or the organization could do (or could have done) to help them be more successful.

Once you have listened to and understand their perspective (even though you may not agree), offer your honest feedback and assessment of the situation. Use concrete examples to support your point of view. Express the fact that you are concerned about their own happiness and well-being. The conversation might lead into a discussion about finding a job that is better suited for their abilities and personality traits.

Playing the role of coach and demonstrating a true care and concern for them as a person might lead to a great outcome. You are in a great position to be able to offer them helpful feedback in terms of what you see as their strengths. You may be able to reposition them in the organization or provide them some leads for other jobs outside of your organization. You may be able to refer them to a certain training program, employment agency, or job coach. If they do choose to resign, the win–win is that you have the opportunity to hire the right person and you have shown respect for the individual. That individual is less likely to badmouth you and the organization. From their standpoint, they have a chance for a fresh start in a position that is better suited for them. They have the opportunity to be less stressed and happier.

SUMMARY

Reaching a win–win outcome from a challenging and difficult conversation is not easy and not always achievable. As with any interaction between one or more individuals, it can be complicated. What you may see as a win–win solution may not be viewed that way by the other party. Think of it in terms of communicating the outcome to parties outside of the situation or organization. If the result of the conversation were turned into a news article or report, would the general public view it as a win–win? Would an unbiased, reasonable person see the outcome as reasonable and as a case where both parties benefited as a result of the conversation?

Despite the unknown, the complexity, and the uniqueness of each situation, it is still important to approach the conversation with a win–win mindset. It is well worth the effort to carefully consider what a successful win–win might be for everyone involved. Honoring and respecting individuals' own desires and needs is never a bad thing and has the potential to pay great dividends.

CHAPTER 10 RECAP

- A win–win outcome from a challenging conversation means that both parties have been respected and heard, and it creates a mutually beneficial outcome.

- Pursuing a win–win solution is an admirable and essential goal of a meaningful conversation and relationship.
- There are standards of conduct that should be followed when entering a difficult conversation with win–win as a desired outcome: 1) Respect and care for the other party; 2) adhere to the principles of good conversation; 3) agree to keep the conversation going; and 4) summarize at the end of the meeting.
- There are strategies that can be employed to improve the chances of a win–win outcome: 1) Agree to standards of conduct; 2) focus on the issues; 3) figure out the perspective of the other party; 4) think outside the box; and 5) know your fallback position.
- Win–win may not always be possible, but it is the best mind-set as you approach a challenging situation.

Chapter Eleven

Embrace Every Opportunity

Every experience is an opportunity to learn and grow.

—Anonymous

Based on what you have learned, it is time to embrace every challenge and every opportunity and become a better conversationalist. We can all improve the way we handle our interactions with others. The principles are not always easy to implement, but they are worthy of serious consideration. It is hard work to navigate the complexities of interactions, conversations, and relationships, but it will always be worth the time, hard work, and extra effort.

THE ART OF CONVERSATION

Conversation is an art and not a science. There is no perfect formula that you can follow to guarantee a positive, meaningful experience as a result of a challenging conversation. There are many uncontrollable variables that make it impossible to predict. Just like art, conversations require some preplanning. Artists typically think about what they want to create. They make sure they have adequate time to work on the project. Part of their preplanning requires them to make sure they have the right materials, the materials that are appropriate for the masterpiece they are attempting to create.

A great, well-thought-out idea and plan; enough time to create; and the right materials are essential to a successful creation. The creator is also flexible as they begin to work on the project. Many artists begin to create with a certain idea in mind only to adjust the project as it develops.

Sometimes the result is much different than the original intent. Sometimes the outcome is much better than expected. Other projects turn out in ways that are unanticipated and not pleasing to the artist's eye. The artist certainly does not begin the work thinking it is going to be a failure. And failure typically does not stop them from trying again.

The conversation is similar to artwork. There is no guarantee that the outcome will be a beautiful piece of artwork; however, it does not mean that the attempt should not be made. There is always the chance of a great outcome.

Just like the artist, there are things the initiator of the conversation can do to minimize the risk of an undesirable outcome. You need to make sure there has been some preplanning. Planning involves figuring out what a successful outcome looks like. In other words, if all goes perfectly, what does it look like?

Part of preplanning includes making sure you have the right materials or elements. Make sure you are aware of, understand, and are committed to following the principles of good conversation. An artist embraces the project and accepts the challenge, not wanting to miss out on a masterpiece. With conversation, the same things apply. Do not avoid the opportunity. If you embrace it, the result may be a positive outcome. It may result in a great new relationship.

As the artist is working on the project, they are focused on the task at hand. They are not thinking about other things. In a conversation you need to be focused on the interaction and not thinking about other things. Pay attention to the other individual. Focus your attention on what they are saying. Make sure you are actively listening. When you speak, speak carefully and with empathy.

Throughout the process the creator slows down to pay careful attention to every detail. They pay attention to timing. They may step away for a time based on how they are feeling at the moment. They listen to the level of inspiration they are feeling.

The art of conversation is no different. It is wise to slow down during the interaction to make adjustments as necessary. It is important to be sensitive to the timing of the conversation and ever-changing emotions.

Artists continually reflect on every piece of the project. They consider what can be done better. They look for ways to improve the process to ensure a masterful result. In conversation, thoughtful reflection is key. You need to monitor your own behavior. You need to reflect on the other person's behavior as well. Consider how they are feeling based on how they are reacting. You may need to adjust your approach to take their unanticipated behavior into account.

The artist is always focused on that win–win result—creating a masterpiece that brings great satisfaction to the artist, as well as to other individuals who are able to enjoy and admire the project. A win–win in a conversation means you are satisfied with your efforts and the result, as is the other party. It is a beautiful result when both parties are pleased with the outcome.

CONVERSATION IS SIMILAR TO GOLF

The complexity of conversations is similar to the game of golf, more specifically the golf swing. There are many variables that impact the perfect golf swing. Some of these variables are more controllable than others. To fail to acknowledge that these factors exist is a reckless approach to golf. If you ignore these factors, you may hit a good shot, but your chances are not good. It is a haphazard approach that makes no sense. If you can improve your chances of hitting a good shot, why not?

To improve your chances of hitting a good shot, a golf pro will tell you that you need to focus on such things as,

- proper grip pressure on the club
- precise orientation of the club face
- appropriate alignment of hands
- proper distance from the ball
- precise angle of the knees
- correct distance between feet
- proper distribution/redistribution of your weight throughout the swing

And the list goes on. There is a lot to keep in mind just to hit that little ball. If you have all of those things in place, it is likely you will hit the perfect shot. How often does that happen? It happens more often with the golf pros because they devote a great deal of time practicing.

If you do some of the "good swing practices" to some degree or another, you still may hit a good shot. If you do not pay attention to any of them, chances are you will rarely hit a good shot.

The conversation is similar in so many ways. There are many factors that contribute to the success or failure of the outcome of the conversation. Those factors have been described throughout this book. If properly handled and in alignment, you will most likely see amazing results. If some of the factors are in place, you still have a good chance of a positive outcome. If you do not pay attention to any of them, you will most likely not see the results you were hoping for.

Just as golf can be frustrating, so too the art of conversation. There is just too much to think about. There are too many factors that have to work together. In terms of the golf game, continued practice and time spent focused on the desired outcome can result in tremendous enjoyment and satisfaction. Time spent focused on the principles of good conversation, as well as consistently practicing them, will lead to better results and enhanced relationships.

YOU HAVE NOTHING TO LOSE

Artists who create great masterpieces provide items of beauty for the enjoyment of others and satisfaction for themselves. If the artist does not pursue this opportunity for fear of failure, they stand to lose out on the potential for a thing of beauty.

The golf game can bring great entertainment for those who practice and focus on the important aspects of the sport. If the golfer refuses to acknowledge the need to practice and the game's complexity, they miss out on the potential for an enjoyable experience shared with others.

SUMMARY

Engaging in difficult and challenging conversations is hard work. There is so much to think about and consider. It forces you to focus on others and not yourself, it exposes you to a certain amount of vulnerability, and it requires dedicated time and effort. To engage in meaningful conversation has the potential to result in a fulfilling experience. You have nothing to lose and everything to gain by embracing these conversational principles and incorporating them into your daily interactions. A happier, more satisfied, and accomplished you awaits.

Remember, be careful with the words you use, as they will affect your interaction. The interaction creates a conversation. A meaningful and heartfelt conversation builds a positive, rewarding, and significant relationship. Your life will be enriched as your relationships are developed, enhanced, and improved. Keep practicing the principles of good conversation. It is worth the effort.

CHAPTER 11 RECAP

- Conversation is an art and not a science.
- Conversation has a lot of moving parts that need to be addressed to create a successful outcome.
- Practicing the principles, continually and consistently, can lead to better performance.
- Embrace every opportunity to create wonderful, valued, and mutually beneficial relationships through positive interactions and meaningful conversations.

About the Author

Stan H. Wisler is a Pennsylvania Certified School Business Administrator (PCSBA). Since 2005, he has held the position of chief financial officer (CFO) for the Montgomery County Intermediate Unit (an educational service agency) in Norristown, Pennsylvania.

Wisler has worked in school business administration for five different public school districts during the course of twenty-four years prior to accepting his current position as CFO of the Montgomery County Intermediate Unit. He is a past president of the Pennsylvania Association of School Business Officials (PASBO) and the 2017 Gary Reeser Memorial Award recipient, and currently cochairs the PASBO Leadership Development Committee. Wisler is a member of the Professional Development and Editorial committees for ASBO International, as well as author of several articles for *School Business Affairs* magazine and the *PASBO Report*.

He serves as president of the executive board for the School Districts Insurance Consortium (SDIC), a worker's compensation pool for eighty school districts in Pennsylvania. Wisler is also an adjunct professor for Drexel University in their School of Education and a member of the Board of Elders for Faith Church of Worcester, where he also serves as worship leader.

Wisler holds a bachelor of science degree in business administration from Geneva College and an MBA from Villanova University. He and his wife Donna live in Worcester Township, Montgomery County, Pennsylvania. They have three grown children and two granddaughters.

www.ingramcontent.com/pod-product-compliance
Lightning Source LLC
Chambersburg PA
CBHW051815230426
43672CB00012B/2740